TRAVELLERS

LATVIA

By
ROBIN McKELVIE & JENNY McKELVIE

Written and updated by Robin McKelvie and Jenny McKelvie
Original photography by Robin McKelvie

Published by Thomas Cook Publishing
A division of Thomas Cook Tour Operations Limited.
Company registration no. 1450464 England
The Thomas Cook Business Park, 9 Coningsby Road,
Peterborough PE3 8SB, United Kingdom
Email: sales@thomascook.com, Tel: + 44 (0) 1733 416477
www.thomascookpublishing.com

Produced by Cambridge Publishing Management Limited
Burr Elm Court, Main Street, Caldecote CB23 7NU

ISBN: 978-1-84157-896-5

First edition © 2006 Thomas Cook Publishing
This second edition © 2008
Text © Thomas Cook Publishing,
Maps © Thomas Cook Publishing/PCGraphics (UK) Limited

Series Editor: Maisie Fitzpatrick
Production/DTP: Steven Collins

Printed and bound in Italy by Printer Trento

Cover photography: Front L-R: © Gary Woods/Alamy; © Jon Hicks/Corbis;
© Giovanni Simeone/SIME-4Corners Images, Back L-R: © Schmid
Reinhard/SIME-4Corners Images; © Franz-Marc Frei/Corbis.

The paper used for this book has been independently certified as having
been sourced from well-managed forests and recycled wood or fibre
according to the rules of the Forest Stewardship Council.
This book has been printed and bound in Italy by Printer Trento S.r.l.,
an FSC certified company for printing books on FSC mixed paper in
compliance with the chain of custody and on products labelling standards.

FSC

Mixed Sources
Product group from well-managed
forests and recycled wood or fibre

Cert no. CQ-COC-000012
www.fsc.org
© 1996 Forest Stewardship Council

Contents

Introduction

It may only have been an independent nation since 1991, but Latvia has more than made up for lost time ever since and is now a member of both NATO and the EU. One of the fastest-growing economies in Europe is propelling unprecedented change in a country where there are increasingly sharp contrasts between the go-getting capital of Rīga, the wild Baltic coast, the impenetrable pine forests and the sweeping lakes of the east. One Latvia is slick and ultra-modern, bristling with bars and chic clubs, while the other is deeply rural, an intriguing escape overflowing with both organic produce and equally organic experiences; a tension that helps make Latvia such a compelling country to visit.

Latvia is home to not only the biggest and most cosmopolitan city of the Baltic countries, Rīga – dubbed the 'Paris of the North' by Graham Greene – but also a flurry of upcoming towns and cities like the ports of Ventspils and Liepāja. Then there are the richly historical regional centres such as Rēzekne, Jelgava and Bauska, not to mention old-world gems like Kuldīga, Cēsis and Ludzu, three of the country's oldest towns. Even many of Latvia's smaller settlements have their own castle mounds, a sprinkling of attractive churches and old wooden buildings. In the Jelgava region alone there are three world-class palaces.

Then there is the scenery. Latvia boasts an impressive sweep of coastline nearly 500km (311 miles) long, much of it unspoilt, lined with white sandy beaches and backed by rows and rows of

pine trees. In the hinterland rolling hills are transformed into winter ski slopes and fertile plains come complete with old-fashioned farms and picture-postcard perfect wooden buildings. In rural Latvia it often feels like the 20th

The striking gold onion domes of the Church of St Nicholas

Log huts on the picturesque Āraiši Lake in the Vidzeme region

century, let alone the 21st, is yet to dawn. The Latvian countryside is also covered by swathes of native forest where bears, elk and wolves still roam wild.

All the anachronisms of the erstwhile Soviet bloc are rapidly disappearing in urban Latvia. Yes, you may still find the odd Lada on the road and the national diet perhaps veers a little too heavily towards high-fat meat dishes, but changes are afoot. Latvian highways these days are awash with brand-new Mercedes and BMWs, and the country's myriad dining options include everything from fine French eateries and trendy bistros to Thai restaurants and sushi bars. The cultural scene and nightlife are vibrant too. Rīga offers some of the liveliest bars and clubs in Europe, at diverse venues. There is something for everyone – from classical recitals and lounge bars to raucous pubs and dance clubs.

At the same time, there is always somewhere to get away from it all, which is one of the country's greatest charms, whether it be hiding away in a log cabin by a secluded lake in rural Latgale; sunbathing on a secluded stretch of beach in Kurzeme; horseriding in Vidzeme; easing down the Gauja River on a canoe camping safari, pitching your tent and enjoying a night under the stars. Not all your friends may have heard of Latvia, but, no doubt, when you get back from a visit and they see your photos they will be keen to discover for themselves one of Europe's most intriguing countries and great travel secrets.

The land

This tooth-shaped Baltic European country lies between Estonia and Lithuania, bordered by the Baltic Sea on the west, and with Russia and Belarus to the east. One of the smallest countries in Europe, Latvia covers an area of just 64,600sq km (24,942sq miles), and has a lengthy coastline that spans 494km (307 miles).

Geography

Latvia's landmass is mainly flat plain, of which around 30 per cent is arable land. Ten per cent of the country is covered in peat bogs and over 40 per cent is forested. Latvia is awash with inland waterways – it has more than 2,000 lakes and 12,500 rivers and streams.

Climate

Spring and summer

Most people visit Latvia between June and September, when day temperatures regularly rise above 15°C (59°F), frequently going up to the mid-20s (high 70s) in July and August.

Autumn and winter

Although winters can be wet and grey, a visit between December and February is likely to be rewarded with magical snow-covered landscapes. Latvians will tell you how the country is feeling the impact of global warming, experiencing less snowfall in recent years.

Flora and fauna

Around 1,600 types of plants and 1,400 animal and insect species thrive in the country. Over 190 varieties of birds breed in Latvia, with many more passing through on migration routes. Latvia's waters are rich in fish, and grey seals and dolphins can also be spotted along the Baltic coast.

Regions

Kurzeme, in the west, is a sparsely populated area with lots of farmland and an extensive coastline.

Zemgale, in the country's fertile central belt, has traditionally been one of the country's most prosperous areas.

To the south, Latgale is Latvia's poorest and yet one of its most beautiful regions. There are vast swathes of unspoilt countryside and it is also home to a large Russian population.

Vidzeme boasts a landscape similar to that of Latgale, but with the added attraction of a windswept Baltic Sea coast.

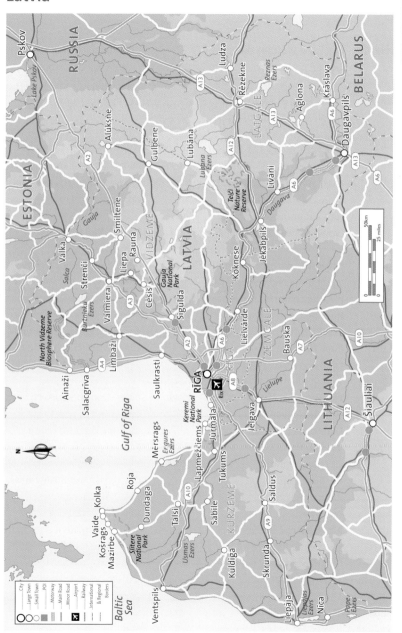

History

9000 BC Latvia's earliest inhabitants arrive.

2000 BC Early Baltic or proto-Baltic people – the Couronians, Latgallians, Selonians, Semgallians and Livs – begin to settle on Latvia's Baltic coast. As the tribes become more culturally aligned, they adopt the collective name Latvians.

AD 1190 Christian missionaries from Germany spend the next two decades trying to impose their religion on Latvia.

1201 Pope Innocent III commands German crusaders, under Bishop Albert von Buxhoeveden of Bremen, to conquer Latvia. The invading Catholic forces settle in modern-day Rīga, and the city plays a pivotal role in the German domination of the Baltics over the next 700 years. Latvian citizens are often deemed inferior to German immigrants; and their trading and property rights are restricted.

1270 The Livonian Order of Knights and the Catholic Church establish the state of Livonia, which encompasses the territory of present-day Latvia and Estonia.

1282 Rīga joins the mighty pan-Baltic trading organisation, the Hanseatic League, becoming a vital link on the east-west trade route.

1521 Latvia's Protestant Reformation begins, but the region of Latgale remains Catholic.

1558 Moscow seeks access to the Baltic Sea and initiates the Livonian Wars, which last for a quarter of a century.

1561 Poles conquer southern Latvia and govern Latgale until the late 18th century.

1629 Sweden occupies a large part of Latvia, which includes Rīga. The Latvian capital is now the biggest city in the Swedish kingdom.

1640 The Duchy of Courland, part of Polish Latvia, colonises the Caribbean island of Tobago and Gambia.

1710 Russia, Poland, Denmark and Sweden are embroiled in the Northern War (1700–21) and Swedish-occupied Latvia falls to Russia.

1768 Ernst Glück becomes the first person to translate the Bible into Latvian.

1782 Rīga basks in a period of cultural and intellectual enlightenment; the city celebrates the opening of its first theatre.

1790 Continued Russian expansionism sees the Polish-ruled region of Latvia come under Russian control. Latvia enters a period of rapid industrialisation.

1812 Fearing that Napoleon's troops will soon march into the city, Rīga's Governor General calls for defensive action and the wooden houses that crowd the city's suburbs are burned to the ground. Ironically, Napoleon and his army never arrive.

1817 Serfdom is outlawed in Rīga and Latvia's industrialisation continues at pace.

1822 The first Latvian newspaper is printed, highlighting a growing sense of national identity within the country.

1873 The growing national consciousness acts as a catalyst to the 'Latvian Awakening' movement, a period when many Latvians rally against the German and Russian influences that dominate society.

1905 After 70 people die during the violent suppression of a political protest, the country goes on strike. In October the strike spirals out of control and around 100 wealthy Germans are murdered. Desperate to end the strike, Russian troops exact a violent revenge, killing more than 1,000 people who participated in the riots. Thousands more are banished to Siberia. Scant regard is given to innocence and guilt.

1914 World War I breaks out in Europe and Germans occupy the western part of the country. As a result, more than two million Latvians become refugees.

1918 As World War I draws to a close, Latvia is divided up between Germany and Russia. Later in the year the defeat of the Germans sees Latvia declare its independence. This is not recognised by the Soviets, who battle to keep control of the country.

1920 Latvia and the Soviet Union finally sign a peace treaty that affords the country its hard-won independence.

1921 Latvia becomes a member of the League of Nations.

1934 Like the rest of Europe, Latvia finds itself in the throes of the post-war depression. Almost ten years of economic depression spark a political coup. This is ultimately a disaster for the country as its democratic government is replaced by an autocratic regime.

1935 The Freedom Monument is erected in Rīga. This symbol of Latvian independence later comes to signify the country's longing for self-rule in Soviet times.

1939 Hitler and Stalin sign the Molotov–Ribbentrop agreement, a pact that, as they carve up the map of Europe, gives the Baltic states to Russia.

1940 Latvia is overrun by Russian troops and the new administration quickly begins to deport thousands of Latvian intellectuals and dissidents to Central Asia and Siberia. Other political prisoners are simply murdered by firing squads. Parts of Kurzeme hold out against both the Germans and the Russians until the end of the war.

1941 Nazi Germany occupies Latvia. Thousands of Latvian Jews are incarcerated and exterminated in concentration camps at Salaspils (*see p45*) near Rīga and elsewhere around the country.

1945 Soviet forces liberate Rīga. As they flee, German soldiers raze everything to the ground. Fearing Russian rule as much as the Nazis, many of the city's residents flee.

1949 Ten years scarred by war, mass murder, deportation and exile leaves Latvia with a severely depleted population, standing at just 65 per cent of the 1939 level.

1956 Latvian rebels finally give up their goal of evicting the Soviets from Latvia and their 16-year rural struggle comes to an end.

1988 A year marked by the first open political protests against the Russian leadership witnesses a 5,000-strong crowd commemorating the deportation of their fellow citizens. Later in the year, more than 10,000 people gather to express their dissent on the anniversary of the Hitler–Stalin Pact. The Popular Front of Latvia, which campaigns for national freedom, is founded.

1989 Latvia holds its first free election. Later that year, half a million people gather on the banks of the Daugava River in Rīga, to celebrate the independence that was first won in 1920.

1991 After the death of five innocents in Rīga's Bastejkalns Park (shot by Soviet soldiers) in January, the vast majority of Latvians (74 per cent) vote for independence from Russia on 3 March. Latvia formally declares its independence in August, and this is rapidly recognised by countries around the globe. Latvia joins the UN.

1992 Latvia adopts a new democratic constitution.

2001 Rīga celebrates its 800th anniversary.

2004 Latvia joins NATO in March and the European Union (EU) in May.

2005 US President Bush makes his first visit to Latvia, extolling its virtues and the manner in which it has managed to secure its independence and develop its economy.

2006 Latvia hosts the 70th IIHF World Ice Hockey Championships, its first major global sporting event. Latvia also hosts major NATO summits.

2007 Presidential elections see Valdis Zatlers replace Vaira Vīķe-Freiberga after an 8-year reign.

Latvian revolution

As the Berlin Wall crumbled and the Iron Curtain lifted all across the Soviet bloc in the late 1980s, the writing on the wall became clear for Latvia and its fellow Baltic states. For four decades the Latvian people had been suppressed by the Soviet Union and embroiled in its attempts to rival the West during the Cold War. Now the road lay open for Latvia to become independent again, for the first time since World War II. It was a road with a lot of potential hazards, though, and with the real possibility of the kind of armed struggle and bloodshed that was unfolding further south in Yugoslavia.

As the Latvian people and the independence movement pushed towards greater freedom, a back-pedalling Mikhail Gorbachev – the Soviet leader who had bravely initiated 'glasnost' and 'perestroika' – scrambled to keep strategic Latvia and its Baltic siblings within the rapidly dissolving Soviet Union. Matters reached a head in 1991 and the focus was, unsurprisingly, on the nation's capital.

Although the struggle did not become as bloody as in neighbouring Lithuania, hardliners within the Soviet army and its Special Forces did stage an action in Rīga. On the night of 20 January, when much of the global media's attention was focused in the Middle East as the first Gulf War unfolded, fighting broke out right in the heart of the city; Special Forces units attacked the Ministry of the Interior. Amongst the scores of innocent people shot that night, five died of their injuries. The attack, as many Latvians feared, did not lead to

Soldiers guard Latvia's Freedom Monument

a major military intervention as Gorbachev, perhaps in the face of strong international criticism, chose to back off.

Latvia was not out of the woods yet, however, despite a referendum in March 1991 when a 73.7 per cent vote for independence seemed to present Moscow with a *fait accompli*. In August that year, as shadowy elements within the Soviet military moved to stage a coup, Special Forces troops ominously appeared on the streets of Latvia again, and brushed aside peaceful protestors and made for the Latvian Parliament. More bloodshed seemed imminent, but these events in Latvia were overtaken by those back in Russia as the anti-Gorbachev coup failed spectacularly. The army and Kremlin hardliners had failed to sideline Gorbachev and his domestic problems and this meant that the Baltic states slipped down his priority list. Finally, Moscow relented and the inexorable move towards independence culminated in September 1991, with first the USA (on 2 September) and then the Soviet Union (on 6 September) recognising Latvian independence. Today the simple but poignant memorials in Bastejkalns Park pay homage to the victims of the struggle to break free from Soviet rule.

Anatol Lieven, in his landmark tome, *The Baltic Revolution*, covers the build-up to independence, as well as the events of January 1991 and the aftermath, with an impressive amount of detail. Lieven's account, though considered controversial in some quarters, offers the best introduction for first-time visitors to Latvia.

The story of Latvia

Politics

Latvia's declaration of independence in 1991 returned self-governance to the country, which it had not enjoyed since World War II. Emancipation from Soviet rule was accompanied by a rise in national pride and an explosion in the number of national political parties. A new satversme (constitution) was rapidly put into place, championing the freedoms and rights of the Latvian people, and to the detriment, as some people believe, of its sizeable Russian minority (see pp100–1).

Political system

The Republic of Latvia has a parliamentary democracy with separate executive, legislative and judicial branches. The Prime Minister and his/her appointed body of Ministers, and the President, comprise the executive. Presidential elections take place once every four years, with the Prime Minister appointed by the incumbent President. The single legislative chamber, the Saeima (parliament), has 100 seats and its members are elected for a four-year term. The Saeima is also responsible for the election of the judiciary, and for appointing Supreme Court judges who oversee the country's legal system. All Latvian citizens over the age of 18 are eligible to vote.

Political parties

Latvian independence saw an explosion in the number of political parties operating in the country. In the country's 2006 election there were candidates from 19 parties, although only seven parties actually won seats.

Russians living in Latvia

Around 25 per cent of Latvia's population are ethnic Russians (661,000 people in 2005); yet, after the country regained its independence in 1991, only those living in Latvia from before World War II and their descendants have been granted citizenship automatically. Other post-war immigrants have to pass exams in the Latvian language and demonstrate their knowledge of Latvian history. For many Russians this poses a significant barrier, while others simply resent the system; as a result, 424,000 people living in Latvia in 2005 did not have citizenship. The country's EU membership in 2004 disadvantaged its stateless residents even further as they, unlike Latvian citizens, are prevented from travelling freely or working elsewhere in the EU (*see pp100–1*).

THE GREAT BANKING COLLAPSE

On gaining independence Latvia set about reforming its banking system, a move that led to rapid privatisation of banks, mergers and new legislation. In a bid to stimulate competition, regulatory laws were lax, particularly with regard to lending money. An audit of the system in late 1994 culminated in the collapse of four of the country's banks (a result of mismanagement, poor accounting, inadequate legislation and corruption) a year later, and the loss of around 40 per cent of Latvia's banking assets and liabilities. While all three Baltic states suffered banking crises in the 1990s, the one experienced by Latvia was the most severe.

Latvian, Rīgan and EU flags fly proudly in Rīga

Economy

Soviet legacy

The Soviet legacy in Latvia was a flagging national economy, as a result of decades of state interference and mismanagement. Back in 1991 analysts expressed concern about the country's ability to survive without its close trading links with Russia.

Post independence

Within 13 years, despite some setbacks along the way, Latvia managed to transform its economy into a profitable market-based system that was accepted into the fold of the EU in 2004. Foreign investment has been positively encouraged and the country's now privately owned industries are thriving – especially pharmaceuticals, electrical appliances, electronics, textiles and the manufacture of agricultural machinery and cars. Dairy products, distilling, shipbuilding and tourism are other key elements of the country's economy. Russia and the other Baltic states remain its largest trading partners, but EU membership has helped Latvia expand its trade links in Europe. By 2007 some economists were starting to warn there was a serious danger of the economy overheating (GDP growth in 2006 was above 11 per cent); fears generated at least in part by spiralling house prices, particularly in Rīga.

WORLDWIDE RECOGNITION

The year 2004 was a big one for Latvia. In the space of just a few months, the country joined both the European Union and NATO. This would have been unthinkable in the years of Soviet rule and many Latvians are still struggling to cope with the rapid pace of development, especially the large Russian 'non-citizen' minority. The final symbolic cementing of Latvia's new place in the European family of nations came when it was given the right to host a NATO summit in 2006, with 26 heads of state in attendance.

The dying Livs?

The community of Livs is very much a part of the history of Latvia. Though they numbered over 2,000 during the 19th century, and held sway over large areas of the Baltic coast, today just a handful of Liv speakers attempt to keep the Liv (*Livod* in their language) culture and traditions alive. Ethnically different from the Latvians, the Livs are a Finno-Ugric people with links to both the coastal Estonians and the Finns (the latter link has been properly explored only in the last decade or so). The Livs prospered in small communities (living in free-standing homesteads) along the Baltic Sea coast, fishing and hunting seals in the winter, since the last ice age. At one time their influence was so strong that 13th-century German crusaders named their newly conquered territory Livonia.

Over the centuries, though, Liv society was eroded and suppressed by the combined domination of Latvian, Russian and German languages and

A traditional house on the Livonian coast

The Livonian flag fluttering in the traditional Livonian heartland

once dying culture, whether just to study it or to work with the language to write their own stories and poems. Liv rights have been enshrined in Latvian law and they now even have the right to announce Livonian as their official nationality in their passports. Seven years after independence, in 1998, the first Livonian Culture Day was celebrated in Mazirbe (it is now an annual event each August). There is also a dedicated Liv cultural centre in Mazirbe (*see p63*). Tourist interest is also starting to help ensure the survival of Liv culture as visitors bring money into the Liv homeland in coastal Kurzeme.

cultures. As the indigenous culture waned, young people left to seek a new life away from the coast. This process reached a crisis point under Soviet rule in the second half of the 20th century, when the traditional Liv heartland of Kurzeme was heavily militarised by the Red Army and their fishing rights were threatened.

In the years following independence there has been something of a resurgence of interest in the Livs, locally known as the 'Awakening', as Latvians in general have started to re-examine their country and its disparate elements. There is now a Liv language newspaper, the *Livli*, and students are being encouraged to delve into this

Despite these positive developments, only a handful of people actually still speak Livonian as their first language and only 100 people have taken the step of declaring themselves Livonian on their passports.

If you have your own vehicle, travelling along the Livonian coast is easy. There is a sprinkling of old fishing villages to explore. You can also walk around old Liv villages that were built behind sand dunes to protect them from the ravages of the Baltic Sea, and see the old abandoned piers from where their fishing boats once busied around. (For more information on the Livonian coast see pp62–3.)

Culture

A cultural renaissance accompanied Latvian independence in 1991, with Latvian theatre, drama and literature rising to the fore. The latter even has a centre dedicated to its preservation, the Latvian Literature Centre (www.literature.lv). For many Latvians, however, nothing expresses their national identity quite as much as music and dance.

Architecture

Latvia's early residents tended to live in small clusters of thatched wooden buildings, with each structure often fulfilling a different function. Examples of this ancient architecture can still be found in the countryside, but they are few and far between. The easiest access to these old homesteads is in Rīga's Open Air Museum, the country's greatest showcase of architecture, with everything from Art Nouveau to modern concrete and steel skyscrapers.

Buskers in Rīga entertain tourists in the Old Town

Art

Mark Rothko, who was born in Latvia and lived in Daugavpils until he was 10 years old, is often held up as one of Latvian's most interesting artists. His post-World War II paintings are commonly regarded as emblems of the country's yearning for political freedom. Regarding art as a tool of socialist propaganda, the Soviet authorities forbade free expression in this area; hence many artists went underground, including the painter Georgs Šēnbergs and the sculptor Zenta Logina.

Dance

Latvians adore the ballet, and dancers like Inese Dumpe, Viktorija Jansone and Marians Butkevičs have all achieved worldwide acclaim. Each year the Latvian capital hosts the International Baltic Ballet Festival (*see p20*). Another important event on the dance calendar is the Sudmaliņas International Folk Dance Festival, which strives to keep alive and promote traditional Latvian dancing.

Literature

Until the mid-16th century, folk songs and stories were the sole vehicle of Latvian literature, with the language kept alive by this largely oral tradition. A Latvian translation of the Lord's Prayer dating back to 1530 heralded an era that saw religious texts dominate the literary scene for 200 years. Scientific works and folk literature dominated the 18th century, while nationalist literature came to the fore in the mid-1800s. Novelists, poets and short-story writers began to emerge later in the 19th century, a period that saw the emergence of one of the country's most significant authors, Jānis Rainis (*see p121*).

Music

Latvia's diverse musical taste encompasses everything from folk and religious music to opera, rock and pop. Every year the capital plays host to the International Organ Music Festival and the Rīga Opera Festival (*see p21*), amongst others. Latvian opera has spawned stars like Inese Galante, Sonora Vaice and Egils Siliņš. In 1926, the country's first (and largest) symphony orchestra, the Latvian National Symphony Orchestra, was established. The Liepāja Symphony Orchestra is also highly regarded.

Folk music is dear to many Latvians, and the call for independence in 1990 which came after the country hosted the Pan Baltika Folk Festival (*see p21*) is often referred to as the 'Singing Revolution'. The oldest rock music festival in Latvia is Liepājas Dzintars (*see p21*), and one of the country's proudest moments came in 2002 when Latvia won the Eurovision Song Contest (*see p20*).

Traditional Latvian wooden architecture

Festivals and events

Latvia boasts an amazingly eclectic range of festivals, from straightforward religious celebrations to musical events involving all the popular genres. Summer is the busiest season, when warmer temperatures bring out the crowds.

March/April
Easter Market
Before they were converted to Christianity Latvians used to celebrate Lieldienas (Day of Light) during the spring equinox. Today, hand-painted and commercially produced eggs and Easter bunnies are a ubiquitous part of Easter festivities. The Easter market on Rīga's Doma Laukums (Cathedral Square) and church services allow visitors to take part in the celebrations.

April
International Baltic Ballet Festival
First hosted in 1996, the festival was initially conceived to celebrate the traditional dances of the Baltic states. It rapidly expanded in popularity and size, attracting performers from around Europe and even as far afield as the USA. The ballet evenings see soloists and dance troupes take to the stage, and the festival has adopted the motto 'From Classical to Avant-garde'. Seminars, exhibitions, children's ballet and music concerts also form essential parts of the festival.
Tel: 6733 6123. www.ballet-festival.lv

June
Gadatirgus
This annual arts and crafts fair graces venues around Rīga, with both traditional and more contemporary arts and crafts on display and for sale.

Valmiera Rock Music Festival
This outdoor event attracts party-goers from all over Latvia and neighbouring

TAKING EUROVISION SERIOUSLY
While much of Europe dismisses the annual Eurovision Song Contest as a cheesy talentless show, Latvians take it a lot more seriously. This comes as no surprise when you consider that this is a nation of public song festivals. Latvia's crowning glory came in 2002 when its entry, the pop number *I Wanna* by Marie N, won the competition. The following year, the 48th Eurovision Song Contest was held in Rīga, much to the delight of the Latvians.

Baltic states, with performances ranging from soft and hard rock to hip hop.
www.valmiera.lv

Baltic Medieval Festival

During this weeklong festival, actors and musicians seek to bring the region's medieval history alive. Previous events have included military parades, jewellery-making workshops, folk concerts and jousting by medieval knights. (Usually second week of June.)
www.balticmedieval.info

Līgo Diena (Midsummer Festival)

Latvia's biggest celebration, this festival sees city dwellers flock to the countryside for an orgy of singing, dancing, drinking and eating around bonfires. (Eve of Jānu Diena – St John's Day.)

Rīgas Operas Festivāls (Rīga Opera Festival)

This ten-day event, which proudly claims to be the first and biggest opera festival in Eastern Europe, is an extravaganza of first rate performers from around the globe who bring to life the masterpieces of Handel, Verdi, Tchaikovsky, Puccini and others.
Tel: 6707 3845. www.opera.lv

July

Rīga Summer Festival

The melodies of chamber and symphony orchestras emanating from various locations pervade the capital's streets during summer.

Jūrmala Pop Festival

A flurry of rock and pop bands lends the seaside resort an additional vibrancy for five days. The acts are mainly Latvian, although some international bands do appear, including some from the other Baltic states and Russia.
www.jurmala-festival.com

Pan Baltika Folk Festival

This large-scale folk festival showcases the traditional music of Latvia, Estonia and Lithuania, and is hosted by Rīga once every three years.

Sigulda Opera Festival

Open-air stages in the ancient city of Sigulda play host to national and international opera performances.
www.lmuza.lv/sigulda

Festival of Ancient Music

Be sure to catch a performance of baroque and Renaissance dance and music during the festival. The spectacular venues include Bauska Castle. (Third weekend in July.)

August

Liepājas Dzintars (Liepāja Amber)

Another annual rock festival, which takes place in Liepāja.
www.liepajasdzintars.lv

September

Arsenāls

Cinemas around Rīga proudly host the country's annual film festival. (Mid-September.) *www.arsenals.lv*

Impressions

Many travellers to Latvia harbour some old stereotypes about the country that date back to the Cold War years. There are in reality no particular difficulties when travelling to and around this increasingly modern European nation. Few travellers will suffer from culture shock, the weather can be an attraction in itself year round and getting around is a fairly straightforward experience. Much that once made Latvia a difficult place to visit has gone, through there are a few charming anachronisms that still await first-time visitors.

When to go

Peak season

Most people visit Latvia between May and September. The peak tourist months are July to August, when the mercury can rise well above 20°C (68°F). At this time the resorts along the Baltic coast can be busy, as Latvians take their summer holidays, although the rest of the country is relatively quiet. Another consideration might be slightly higher hotel prices and more expensive flights during the summer months. Latvia has an average 5–8 days of rainfall every month; however, October is often wetter.

Winter

From December to February Latvia is very cold, with temperatures staying below 0°C (32°F) and snowfall in the inland regions. The festive cheer around Christmas and New Year, combined with the snow-covered ground, can make a visit at this time of the year rewarding.

Latvia's striking Baltic coast

The magnificent Rundāle Palace in the Zemgale region

What to see

Rīga is a destination in itself, so set aside as much time as possible for this historic and captivating city, with its majestic churches, cobbled squares and frenetic entertainment. Just outside Rīga the beach resorts and health spas of Jūrmala are alluring destinations with their Baltic Sea beaches and energetic nightlife in summer.

Stretching to Kurzeme proper to the west, up to the mystical Cape Kolka, the coast is relatively unspoilt and wild. The Livonian coast is compelling for its Liv history and sprinkling of attractive villages. Kurzeme also boasts the rising urban stars of Ventspils and Liepāja, vibrant port cities that have award-winning beaches.

In central Latvia the Zemgale region is renowned for its world-class palaces; if you have the time, try to cover the trio of Rundāle, Mežotne and Jelgava, as well as Bauska's hulking castle ruins and the prosperous city of Jelgava.

Following the mythical Daugava River east into Latgale you enter the 'Land of Blue Lakes', an unspoilt oasis of looming forests and shimmering lakes. This is a good place to get active on foot, or to travel on a bike or by ferry.

In the northernmost region of Vidzeme is the Gauja National Park, famous for its attractive scenery. This is a hub for adventure sports, though there is a sprinkling of castles and museums too for those culturally inclined. The historic towns of Sigulda and Cēsis here are also worth a visit, as are some of the provincial centres and a sweep of the Baltic Sea coast, with resort beaches to the south near Rīga and wilder stretches north towards the Estonian border.

Trams are a regular feature of Latvian cities

Latvia may not be the biggest country in Europe, but there's lots to see and do, so make sure you give yourself enough time to take it all in.

What to take

Rīga is a thriving city where shops sell items similar to those you can buy at home. Shopping around to find those forgotten items can be time-consuming, though, and the choice is very limited away from the capital.

Pack for the weather

Latvia's weather is unpredictable even in the summer. A waterproof jacket, or umbrella, is essential. Evening temperatures are significantly lower than those during the day, so carry a jacket if you are visiting during spring and summer, and a thick, warm coat during the rest of the year. Suntan lotion, sunglasses, a sunhat and mosquito repellent are all useful summertime items.

Essentials

Packing an adequate supply of prescription medication, replacement contact lenses, contact lens cleaning solution, a spare pair of glasses, camera film and spare batteries is a good idea. Don't forget to carry a round two-pin European plug adaptor and to make sure that your mobile telephone is enabled for roaming and has enough credit if you intend to use it.

What to wear

Latvians in cities tend to dress immaculately, and even when they are wearing jeans and trainers they try to ensure that these are clean and look new.

In upmarket restaurants smart casual wear is acceptable, although you might want to pack a jacket and tie for a very special meal. Formal attire is essential for anyone doing business in Latvia.

Annoyances
Background music

Wherever you dine in Latvia, pop songs of the 1980s, Russian dance music or Latvian folk music are likely to come as a dubious accompaniment to your meal. Even the more expensive restaurants have been known to blast loud and inappropriate music.

Cultural differences

Latvia's culture is not dissimilar to that of most western nations, but a few things may take a bit of getting used to.

Smoking

Smoking is banned in all public buildings, including nightclubs and on public transport. Like many countries across the EU, from July 2008 smoking will not be permitted in cafés, restaurants, etc.

Alcohol

Heavy drinking is an inherent part of the Latvian culture and it is not unusual to see people ordering beer in cafés or restaurants at breakfast time. You may also see groups of people drinking on the streets at any time of day. This is something that is beginning to change, however, with the younger generation of health- and image-conscious Latvians.

Driving

Latvia's roads are mostly quiet outside the cities. On busy roads, however, Latvian drivers tend to be rash, overtaking erratically and forcing oncoming cars to brake sharply. Other drivers accept these rash manoeuvres and you will rarely hear the honking of horns or see lights flashed in anger, which makes it all the more frustrating when someone beeps their horn behind you because they think you are driving too slowly (*see pp179–80*).

One of the biggest shocks to people who travel around Latvia for the first time is the fact that a large number of the country's roads, even highways, are not sealed. Instead, road surfaces are often made from compacted mud or gravel. This doesn't deter fast drivers who leave a storm of dust and flying stones in their wake. Projects are now under way to improve the condition of the roads, which suffered as a result of decades of underinvestment by the Soviet-era authorities.

Rural life

If you venture south into the Latgale region of the country you may well

The old Rīga skyline, with the castle centre-stage

Kurzeme woman

encounter women leading their cows alongside the edge of the road, and people transporting milk cans on cycles, or horse-drawn ploughs. This region of Latvia is the poorest and here bicycles are the most common form of transport.

Derelict factories

When the USSR took control of Latvia in 1945, it decided to make the country a centre of industry, building factories in many towns and importing thousands of Russian workers to man them. Many of the factories have long since closed but their legacy remains, and you will find smokeless chimneys, rusting pipelines and crumbling factory buildings on the outskirts of many Latvian towns. Another blot on Latvia's landscape is the Soviet-style housing blocks built to accommodate factory workers: fortunately, however, these tend to be low-rise.

Customs and traditions

Centuries after their conversion to Christianity, many Latvians still observe some pagan traditions, such as raking over gravel paths in public cemeteries to prevent the spirits of the deceased from following you home. In preparation for Jānu Diena (St. John's Day) Latvians give their homes and gardens an overhaul, digging up weeds, removing cobwebs and laundering clothes. It is also a time for brewing homemade beer. Christianity has brought important customs of its own, notably the celebration of name days.

Getting around

Public transport

Most of Latvia's villages, towns and cities can be easily explored on foot. Rīga has a good network of local buses, trams and trolleybuses. It is possible to travel between towns and cities by train and bus, but to get off the beaten track you will need to hire a car. (For information on car hire see p179.)

NOT SO GAY RĪGA

Those who thought Latvia did not suffer from homophobia were rudely awakened in 2005. After conservative and extremist groups subjected the authorities to a barrage of criticism for giving permission for the first ever 'Gay Pride March' in Rīga, the parade was banned two days before the event. The organisers, though, were undeterred and had the decision overturned in court. Fifty hardy souls embarked on the march, but were overcome by hundreds of protestors who gathered on the streets to hurl missiles, spray mace and verbally abuse them.

RĪGA'S RUSSIAN NIGHTLIFE

With a Russian population that is over 30 per cent, it is not surprising that many of Rīga's bars, cafés and restaurants are geared mainly to a Russian clientele. A good example is the Groks Bar (*Kaļķu Iela 22*), a disco with an old Russian train used as the cloakroom, where non-Russians are welcomed at best with steely stares. Nearby is Nostgalicja, a retro Soviet-era café where communist apparatchiks would have felt at home. If you have time to spare, it is worth seeking out a slice of this Russian underbelly that lurks beneath the surface of the bright new Rīga.

Travelling by bicycle

This compact and relatively flat country is ideal for those wishing to travel by bicycle. You can hire bikes in larger towns and resorts like Rīga, Sigulda, Cēsis and Jūrmala, but anyone contemplating a serious amount of cycling should consider bringing their own bike.

If you are planning a bike tour, waterproof clothing and cycle helmets are also a good idea. Many cyclists plan their journeys independently, often combining a jaunt in Latvia with a trip into neighbouring Lithuania and Estonia. It is also possible to join an organised group through travel agents like the Rīga-based Baltic Country Holidays (*www.celotajs.lv*).

Opening times

Tourism has only recently started to take off in Latvia, so opening times are currently subject to regular change. As printed times are likely to be unreliable, we have not included them for the majority of sights featured within this book.

The people

The ethnic mix of Latvia's citizens comes as a surprise to many visitors: just 58 per cent of the population are classed as Latvian, 30 per cent are Russian, 4 per cent Belarussian, 3 per cent Ukrainian and 3 per cent Polish. These diverse people adhere largely to the Lutheran, Roman Catholic and Orthodox faiths.

Taken at face value, the pragmatism of Latvians can sometimes appear aloof or downright unfriendly. Their characteristic reserve often arises from uncertainty or shyness, however; when they make friends Latvians like to believe that they are for life. Many of Latvia's young people are delaying having children, while others are leaving to work overseas; as a result, the country's population is in decline.

A typical Latvian road through the nation's dense forests

Rīga

The city of Rīga has been on a renewed rise ever since Latvia joined the EU and NATO in 2004, three years after the city celebrated its 800th anniversary. Things have seldom looked so rosy for a cosmopolitan capital once revered across Europe as the 'Paris of the North'. Older than both Stockholm and St. Petersburg, Rīga is the only Baltic state capital with a big-city buzz.

It has not always been such good going for Rīga, as throughout its turbulent history it has been routinely sacked, occupied, reoccupied and sacked again, by everyone from the Teutonic Knights and Swedes, through to the French and the Poles. In the 20th century came devastating invasions by the Nazis and Stalin. The Soviets left behind housing estates on the city's periphery that are an eyesore and Stalinist-era architecture, but their traces are gradually being paved over.

The focus of the city, as it has always been, is firmly on the Old Town, which tumbles towards the banks of the Daugava River in a maze of cobbled streets, tall spires and impressive squares. Across Bastejkalns Park lies the New Town, the commercial heart of the city, with its broad avenues, grid-like layout and Art Nouveau façades, while further downriver lies the city's sprawling port. It is ironic that the city that was once besieged and captured by Germany now boasts – after Germany's own World War II devastation – Europe's most impressive array of Germanic Art Nouveau architecture, as recognised by UNESCO on their World Heritage List.

The Baltic Sea is just over 12km (7 miles) away, but Rīga's weather is not as harsh as people might imagine. When the sun shines, the city's numerous parks fill up, tables spill out of cafés and revellers laze along the city's canal in boats, creating an atmosphere that is more Mediterranean than Eastern European.

LANDMARKS
Brīvības Piemineklis (Freedom Monument)

The massive Freedom Monument has a sacred place in the heart and mind of every Latvian. This potent symbol of the nation was erected by the citizens of Rīga in 1935 and somehow managed to survive four decades of Soviet rule. A poignant local joke during the communist era was that the monument

Rīga city map

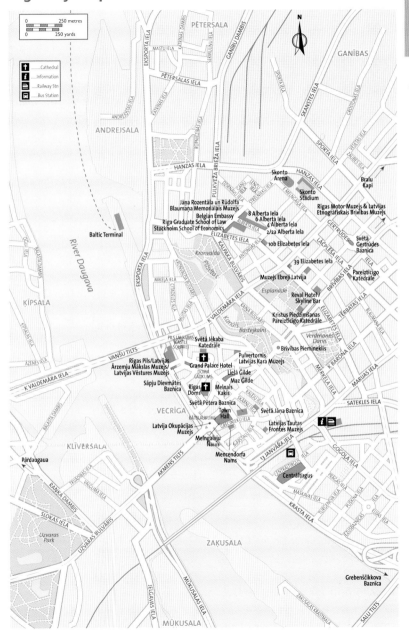

0 250 metres
0 250 yards

- Cathedral
- Information
- Railway Stn
- Bus Station

N

PĒTERSALA

GANĪBAS

EKSPORTA IELA
MASTU IELA
KATRĪNAS DAMBIS
SĒRNIŪNU IELA
GANĪBU DAMBIS

PĒTERSALAS IELA

ANDREJOSTAS IELA

ANDREJSALA

SPORTA IELA

SKANSTES IELA

KRASTMALAS IELA

VESTAS IELA

ZAUBES IELA

RŪPNIECĪBAS IELA

HANZAS IELA

PULKVEŽA BRIEŽA IELA

Skonto
Arena

HANZAS IELA

Brāļu
Kapi

SPORTA IELA

Skonto
Stādi
ons

Rīgas Motor Muzejs & Latvijas
Etnogrāfiskais Brīvbas Muzejs

GERTRŪDES

Baltic Terminal

River Daugava

KĪPSALA

DZIRNAVU IELA
STRĒLNIEKU IELA

Jāņa Rozentāla un Rūdolfa
Blaumaņa Memoriālais Muzejs
Belgian Embassy
Riga Graduate School of Law
Stockholm School of Economics

8 Alberta Iela
6 Alberta Iela
4 Alberta Iela
2/2a Alberta Iela

Svētā
Gertrūdes
Baznīca

LĀČPLĒŠA IELA

ELIZABETES IELA

ALBERTA IELA

10b Elizabetes Iela

39 Elizabetes Iela

Pareizticīgo
Katedrāle

Kronvalda

KALPAKA BULVĀRIS

ANTONIJAS IELA

Muzejs Ebreji Latvija

BRĪVĪBAS IELA

TĒRBATAS IELA

BAUMAŅA IELA

EKSPORTA IELA

KRONVALDA BULVĀRIS

MĪKEĻA IELA

Pilsētas kanāls

Esplanāde

Reval Hotel /
Skyline Bar

K VALDEMĀRA IELA

RAIŅA BULVĀRIS

Kanāls

Bastejkalns

Kristus Piedzimšanas
Pareizticīgo Katedrāle

ELIZABETES IELA

K BARONA IELA

MERĶEĻA IELA

MARIJAS IELA

SATEKLES IELA

Verdmanis
Dārzs

VANŠU TILTS

AZENES IELA

K VALDEMĀRA IELA

BALASTA DAMBIS

PILS LAUKUMS
CASTLE
SQUARE

Svētā Jēkaba
Katedrāle

Pulvertornis
Latvijas Kara Muzejs

Brīvības Piemineklis

Rīgas Pils/Latvijas
Ārzemju Mākslas Muzejs/
Latvijas Vēstures Muzejs

DOMA
LAUKUMS

Grand Palace Hotel

Lielā Ģilde

Maz Ģilde

Sāpju Dievmātes
Baznīca

Rīgas
Doms

Melnais
Kakis

VECRĪGA

Svētā Pētera Baznīca

Town
Hall

Svētā Jāņa Baznīca

Latvijas Tautas
Frontes Muzejs

Latvija Okupācijas
Muzejs

RĀTSLAUKUMS

Melngalvju
Nams

Mencendorfa
Nams

13 JANVĀRA IELA

Centrāltirgus

GOGOĻA IELA

KLĪVERSALA

AKMENS TILTS

MASKAVAS IELA

KRASTA IELA

Pārdaugaua

TRIJĀDĪBAS IELA
VALGUMA IELA

RANKA DAMBIS

SLOKAS IELA

UZVARAS BULVĀRIS

MŪKUSALAS IELA

JELGAVAS IELA

Uzvaras
Park

ZAĶUSALA

Grebenščikkova
Baznīca

ZAĶUSALAS KRASTMALA

SALU TILTS

MŪKUSALA

The Freedom Monument is a proud symbol of
Latvian independence and nationality

PALATIAL LUXURY

Today the Grand Palace (*see p168*) is widely
regarded as Latvia's finest hotel. The lavish
building has a colourful history as it was
designed by the architect J F Baumanis to
house the State Bank back in 1877, and only
since independence has it become a hotel. The
Grand Palace managed to absorb two
surrounding buildings at 7 and 9 Mazâ Pils
Iela in 2000 with the help of London-based
architects Sarma & Norde, without losing any
of its character. A favourite of the rich and
famous, illustrious guests rumoured to have
enjoyed the palatial accommodation include
Catherine Deneuve, the Pet Shop Boys, REM,
Helmut Kohl and Sting.

the five hulking 1930s zeppelin hangars
that now house Rīga's Central Market.
A world away from the glossy shopping
malls, it is possible to rub shoulders
with Rīga's locals here, who come to
snap up cheap fruit and vegetables.
There is also a rabble of stalls outside
the main hangars.

Rīgas Doms (Rīga Cathedral)
The foundations of the city's
cathedral were laid on St Jacob's Day in
1211, by Albert von Buxhoeveden, who
became its first bishop. In the museum
inside there are displays portraying
Rīga between the World Wars, as well
as maps and postcards of Old Rīga.
A highlight is the world-famous organ
crafted in 1883–84 by the German
company Waclker & Co, and decorated
with wooden carvings from the 17th
and 18th centuries.
Doma Laukums. Tel: 6721 3213.
Admission charge.

was like a travel agent, since laying
flowers there guaranteed a one-way
ticket to Siberia.

Centrāltirgus (Central Market)
Visitors wanting to leave the 21st
century behind them should head for

The Cathedral is a highlight of Rīga's Old Town

OLD TOWN

Rīga's pedestrianised Old Town, a riot of cobbled streets, lofty church spires and lavish buildings, is a real joy to explore. Its medieval street plan is easy to follow and its winding cobbled alleyways invite idle wandering, with plenty of cafés and bars on hand for en-route refreshments.

Trio of squares

Rīga's Old Town is home to no less than three impressive public squares: Doma Laukums (Cathedral Square), Pils Laukums (Castle Square) and Rātslaukums (Town Hall Square).

Doma Laukums (Cathedral Square)

Doma Laukums is home to the city's landmark cathedral (*see p30*). It also boasts an array of grand façades that overlook its cobbled expanse, as well as a sprinkling of beer gardens in summer.

Pils Laukums (Castle Square)

In Pils Laukums you will find the castle that is now home to Latvia's President, as well as the **Latvijas Ārzemju Mākslas Muzejs** (Latvian Museum of Foreign Art) and **Latvijas Vēstures Muzejs** (Latvian History Museum).

Rātslaukums (Town Hall Square)

Rātslaukums was painstakingly rebuilt after being severely damaged during World War II. Today it is back to its graceful old self and contains the rebuilt town hall, the **Melngalvju Nams** (House of the Blackheads) and the city's main tourist information office.

The magnificent Doma Laukums

Rīga

Lielā Ǵilde and Maz Ǵilde (Great and Small Guild Houses)

These remnants of the days when the city was a bustling member of the Hanseatic League are still very much part of the fabric of the city on Meistaru. The Gothic Great Guildhall hosts concerts performed by the National Symphony Orchestra, while its smaller sibling is a favourite photo stop for visiting tourists. Look out also for the **Melnais Kaķis** (Black Cat) building opposite the guildhalls, which is surrounded by its own tall tales and urban myths.

Filharmonijas Parks.

Melngalvju Nams (House of the Blackheads)

This stunningly renovated Gothic building on the revamped Rātslaukums dates back to the 14th century. It later became the headquarters of a group of local unmarried merchants: the Blackheads. Badly damaged in World War II, it was completely rebuilt in the 1990s and shines at night when it is floodlit. The mighty gable rises dramatically 28m (92ft) above the square, and the interior is suitably impressive, with a rebuilt hall where the Blackheads would once have met.

Rātslaukums 7. Tel: 6704 4300.
Admission charge.

Pulvertornis (Powder Tower)

This chunky red-brick fortress, one of the oldest buildings in the city, still sports the scars of its troubled history with cannon pockmarks dotting its exterior. This is one of the last intact remnants of the fortifications that once protected Rīga and helped it hold out against various sieges. Today it is home to the **Latvian War Museum** (*see p36*).

Svētā Pētera Baznīca (St Peter's Church)

Another of Rīga's most striking edifices is St Peter's Church, which is dedicated to the city's patron saint. Its unmistakable red-brick style is common to all countries that border the Baltic, from Germany to Estonia. The sturdy church dates back to 1408, when it was built to replace a wooden church on the same site. Its wooden spire, the highest in Europe, was obliterated by German shelling in 1941; today's 122m (400ft) steel replica was completed in 1973. The observation gallery offers sweeping views of the city.

Skārņu Iela 19. Tel: 6722 9426.
Free admission.

A HANDY CARD?

The Rīga Card has been specially designed by the local tourist office for people visiting Rīga on short breaks. The card allows free travel on all trams, buses and trains in Rīga, and also as far as Jūrmala, as well as free or discounted entrance to many museums and cultural attractions. It is available for 24 hours, 48 hours and 72 hours, and can be purchased from travel agents and the main city tourist office (*Rātslaukums 6; tel: 6703 7900; www.rigatourism.com*). You may want to weigh up whether it is good value or not depending on where you want to visit, as most sights are centrally located.

Walk: Rīga Art Nouveau

Rīga is the proud owner of one of the most impressive arrays of Art Nouveau architecture anywhere in the world. This elaborate art form, Jugendstil in German, flourished in the city from the late 19th century through to World War I. A lavish display of buildings lights up the part of the city that lies on the other side of the Freedom Monument from the Old Town.

Distance: 1.5km (1 mile). Time: allow 2 hours.

Start by walking from the Old Town past the Freedom Monument on Brīvības. Take the second left turn onto Kalpalka, and to the beginning of the walk.

1 Kalpalka bulvāris

Once you have crossed the intersection with Valdemāra keep your eyes focused on the left side of the street where

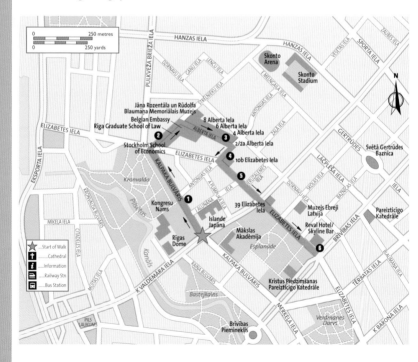

you will see some stunning Art
Nouveau buildings.
*At the junction of Kalpalka bulvāris and
Elizabetes Iela head northeast onto
Strēlnieku Iela, stopping to look at the
yellow building at the right corner.*

2 Strēlnieku Iela

Two enormous classical columns
dominate the street-facing part of the
façade, which is clearly dated 1910.
Stick to the right-hand side of the
street and walk to No 4a, which is
currently occupied by the Stockholm
School of Economics and was designed
by Mikhail Eisenstein, the venerated
Russian-born architect (1867–1921).
This stunning façade features
Eisenstein's characteristic busts, rooftop
statues, geometric lines and wrought-
iron balconies. Next door is the Rīga
Graduate School of Law, another of his
masterpieces.
*Taking the first right turn will bring you
to Alberta Iela.*

3 Alberta Iela

Alberta Iela is a street whose Art
Nouveau architecture is slowly being
restored. The striking building at No 13
houses the Belgian Embassy, another of
Mikhail Eisenstein's designs. The
architect's work is also on display at
Nos 8, 6, 4, 2 and 2a. The rooftop
arches and protective sphinx and
dragons are just some of the ornate
charms of these apartment blocks that
have survived despite years of neglect.
Turn right again to Antonijas Iela.

4 Antonijas Iela

The roaring lions, winged angels and
fair maidens situated above a real-estate
agency are well worth studying.
Turn left at Elizabetes Iela.

5 Elizabetes Iela

Elizabetes Iela is home to many of the
city's finest Art Nouveau buildings.
No 10b is particularly attractive.
Alongside the grand Art Nouveau
architecture you will also spot an old
wooden house at No 39.
*Walk on the left-hand side of Elizabetes
for 600m (660yds) until you reach the
Reval Hotel Latvija.*

6 Skyline Bar

On the 26th floor of the *Reval Hotel
Latvija* is the *Skyline Bar* (*see p148*).
Find a window table and you can
survey the dramatic architecture of
this beautiful city from a height.
*From the main door simply follow Brīvības
for 600m (660yds) in a southwesterly
direction back to the old town.*

Typical Art Nouveau architecture in Rīga

MUSEUMS

Rīga is home to a wealth of important museums, most of them located either in or around the Old Town. Since 1991 a concerted effort has been made to shore up these cultural institutions and invest in a renewed exploration of Latvian culture.

Arzemju Mākslas Muzejs
(Latvian Museum of Foreign Art)

Within the walls of the city's old castle is either a treasure-trove of art from many periods or a confusing hotchpotch, depending on how you look at it. The highlights include artefacts from ancient Greece and Rome, not to mention Egypt, and Central European paintings from the 18th and 19th centuries.
Pils Laukums 3. Tel: 6722 6467.
Free admission.

Latvijas Kara Muzejs
(Latvian War Museum)

The Latvian War Museum is simultaneously one of the most interesting museums in the city and one of the most controversial. Within the 14th-century red-brick Pulvertornis (Powder Tower) are displays covering the various wars that have ravaged the country. There are good sections on the War of Liberation (1918–20), when the Latvians fought off the Soviets and the Germans, and on the Latvian volunteers who served with the German Waffen SS during World War II. There has been much debate on the latter's role in atrocities, and the parades of the surviving veterans are often a source of embarrassment to the government.
Smilšu Iela 20. Tel: 6722 8147.
www.karamuzejs.lv. Free admission.

The Occupation Museum of Latvia covers both the German and Russian occupations of Latvia during the 20th century

Latvijas Okupācijas Muzejs (Occupation Museum of Latvia)

Housed in an unprepossessing communist-era building, the museum takes visitors on a journey through Latvia's turbulent recent history – from the Soviet and Nazi occupations during World War II right up to the events that led to Latvian independence in 1991. If you have even a passing interest in the history of Latvia this is an essential stop. Outside, the statue of Latvian Riflemen remains a subject of much local controversy (*see box*).
Strēlnieku Laukums 1. Tel: 6721 2715.
www.occupationmuseum.lv
Free admission.

Latvijas Tautas Frontes Muzejs (Latvian People's Front Museum)

One of the city's newer museums, this is a compelling place to visit. Housed in a building that was used as a base for some of the key figures in the independence drive in the 1990s, the modest exhibits shed light on the action behind the headlines in those tumultuous days.
Vecpilsētas 13–15. Tel: 722 4502.
Free admission.

Mencendorfa Nams (Mentzendorff House)

Time stands still at this old merchant's house, which was built in the 18th century. The name Mentzendorff relates to the last Baltic German family who lived here and ran their family grocery business. Myriad

HEROES OR VILLAINS?

It is hard to miss the huge statue by the Occupation Museum on the fringes of Rīga's Old Town. It commemorates the 40,000 Latvians who answered the Russian call to take arms against Germany in 1915 and who were collectively known as the *Strēlmieki* (Riflemen). They suffered horrific losses, which some scholars have suggested was because the Russians sacrificed them fearing that they were in effect a Latvian army-in-waiting. Units went on to feature heavily in the Russian Revolution, both on the Bolshevik side and with the Latvian nationalists. In Soviet times they were awarded their own museum, which is ironically now the Occupation Museum, and their role in history still remains a subject of much controversy.

artefacts create a period feel, and temporary art exhibitions brighten up the basement.
Grēcinieku Iela 18. Tel: 6721 2951.
Admission charge.

Muzejs Ebreji Latvija (Museum of Latvia's Jews)

Latvia's Jews were virtually wiped out during World War II, and this modest museum pays tribute to their often forgotten struggle. The Jews had not only the evils of Nazism to deal with but also a communist Russian regime that did not look kindly upon them. The focus of the museum is not just on the tragedy but also the contribution that Jews have made to Latvia over the years.
Skolas Iela 6. Tel: 728 3484.
Free admission.

Rīga

St John's Church lies at the heart of Rīga's Old Town

and admiring it from one of the park benches.
Brivibās Iela 23.
Tel: 6721 1216. Free admission.

Sāpju Dievmātes Baznīca (Church of Our Lady of the Sorrows)

This Roman Catholic church is a relative newcomer, dating from the late 18th century when the Russian Tsar and Polish royalty paid for its completion. Look out for the image of the Virgin Mary at the door as you enter, which came from St Jacob's Church in Rīga.
Lielā Pils Iela 5.
Free admission.

CHURCHES
Kristus Piedzimšanas Pareizticīgo Katedrāle (Orthodox Cathedral)

This lavish Russian Orthodox church dates back to the late 19th century. The design is completely different from that of the city's Protestant churches; it has five gorgeous onion domes and an exterior that gleams in the sunlight. During communist times this ecclesiastical building suffered an inglorious spell as a planetarium, hence the name that many locals still give it: 'the Planetarium'. As the cathedral is restored to its glory many of its icons were brought back and others were donated. The best way to take it all in is by walking around the park at its base

Svētā Gertrūdes Baznīca (St Gertrude's Church)

This vaulting central church is unmistakable with its sweeping church tower, which is topped off with a green spire. The lower spire is awash with all sorts of fanciful architectural touches such as gargoyles. It may not be the most famous and aesthetically pleasing ecclesiastical building in the city, but it is a worthwhile diversion for those with more than a day here.
Gertrūdes Iela. Free admission.

Svētā Jāņa Baznīca (St John's Church)

Another Rigān church with a rich history, St John's was originally home of the Dominicans, but over the centuries fell into the possession of the Lutherans; it once also served as an arsenal for the city. The most notable features of this unheralded church are the impressive 15th-century sculptures of St Peter and St Paul which adorn the 18th-century altar. Legend has it that during the building of St John's a pair of monks were bricked up between the walls to continue their pious life. *Jāņa Iela 7. Tel: 6722 4028. Free admission.*

Svētā Jēkaba Katedrāle (St Jacob's Cathedral)

Just outside the walls of the Old Town, the Roman Catholic cathedral of Rīga has been reincarnated many times. It is easily recognisable due to its vaulting 73m (240ft) spire, the city's third highest. St Jacob's Church was built way back in the 13th century, and, during its eclectic past, has served as a Lutheran parish church, a Jesuit church and even a Swedish garrison church. Now it is an atmospheric place for Catholic worship. A ghoulish story surrounding the church tells of a mysterious body that was found when the north wall was being renovated in the 18th century – no one ever found out who he was or how he died. *Jēkaba Iela 2. Tel: 6732 6419. Free admission.*

An ornate Art Nouveau façade in the Latvian capital

Rīga Black Balsams

To say that Rīga Melnais Balzams (Rīga Black Balsams) is an acquired taste may be something of an understatement, but this potent brew is certainly worth drinking to see what all the fuss is about; the populace of the city seems to love it.

Trying to find out what goes into this alcoholic concoction is not easy, as the exact recipe is a closely guarded secret, one that has been kept within the city since it first resurfaced in the 18th century. Some claim the drink was the brainchild of an experimenting Rīgan pharmacist, Abraham Kunze.

Attempting to pin down its unique flavour can also be a tricky process, though the thick black brew has definite echoes of orange peel, ginger and nutmeg apart from numerous domestic grasses and roots. In all, there are said to be 25 separate ingredients.

The effects of Rīga Black Balsams, beyond the obvious inebriation induced by a stupefying 45 per cent proof alcoholic punch, are said to include the calming of jangled nerves and the settling of stomach ailments, the latter somewhat ironic given its propensity for dealing out lethal hangovers. True Black Balsams aficionados may risk drinking it neat, but most Latvians mix it with soft drinks, most popularly with Coca-Cola.

Trendy bars these days are experimenting with chic cocktails that use other spirits and mixers to offset the bitterness and strong aftertaste of Black Balsams. The most famous place to sample Rīga's finest drink is the original Rīgas Balzams bar at Torņa Iela 4 (see p148) – an

Black Balsams is on sale thoughout Latvia

The brew can be something of an acquired taste

unpretentious cellar/bar/restaurant where you can try it in myriad permutations and combinations. Rīga's Black Balsam is so popular with locals and tourists alike that the city has now opened a second theme bar, B-Bars. This is a more modern and stylish venue for enjoying the age-old drink. B-Bars (*Doma Laukums 2*), replete with leather sofas and posing locals, is a great place to see and be seen. It does very good food too, to mitigate the effects of the alcohol.

Visitors may want to think about taking back a bottle or two – supermarkets are the cheapest place to buy it – as it makes both an unusual souvenir in handmade ceramic jugs and an unusual drink to test dinner-party guests.

Only one company has the right to produce the genuine Rīga Black Balsams, and it has been at it since 1900. In recent years the production methods have been updated and the makers claim that it now lasts much longer in the bottle, making it more attractive for visitors to take it home. So make sure you try it at least once during your stay in Rīga, even if it is heavily disguised in strong coffee or Coca-Cola. The makers even have a website dedicated to the hallowed drink (*www.balzams.lv*), whose qualities have been recognised worldwide with the bestowal of no fewer than 30 awards.

Bastejkalns Park is Rīga's green lung

On warm days, this central green space fills up with gossiping workers, 20-somethings glued to their mobile phones and couples taking lazy strolls along the **Pilsētas Kanāls** (City Canal) that runs through the park. In the darker background, amidst the trees, stand the polished stone memorials to five Latvians who were shot dead near here when the Soviets tried to crush the independence movement in January 1991. The victims included two cameramen and a student.

Esplanāde

This neat 19th-century park is well manicured with trim grass, neatly arranged flowerbeds and a sprinkling of benches where visitors can relax and watch the world go by. The park also houses the **Kristus Piedzimšanas Pareizticīgo Katedrāle** (Orthodox Cathedral) (*see p38*), which was handed back to the church after years of secular use during the Soviet occupation. Besides the cathedral the Esplanāde also houses the Gothic-styled **Academy of Art** and the baroque **National Museum of Fine Arts**.

Kronvalda

Adjacent to Bastejkalns, this park shares the Pilsētas Kanāls with its neighbour. It tends to be a quieter place, with little to see but for the sculptures of the Latvian writer Rūdolfs Blaumanis and composer Alfreds Kalniņš. On busy summer days, therefore, this is a more relaxed place to visit.

PARKS AND THE DAUGAVA RIVER

Although it is the largest city of the Baltic states, Rīga is still a green city with plenty of open spaces where visitors can escape the increasingly busy streets. Even in the centre of the city there are parks and gardens which come into their own from spring right through summer, and are popular venues for bracing strolls in winter.

Bastejkalns Park

Two aspects of modern Rīga can be seen on display in Bastejkalns Park.

Pārdaugava

This large park lies a short tram ride out of the Old Town and is home to the city's **Botanical Garden**. The other main reason to come here is to take in the views of the vaulting church spires of old Rīga.

River Daugava

The wide expanse of the city's lifeblood, the Daugava is hard to miss as it sweeps through the city on its way to the Baltic Sea. In spring and summer tour boats regularly take on the strong currents, opening up unique views of Rīga's Old Town as they go. There are also extended trips seawards to the beachfront resorts of Jūrmala, which take in the city's sprawling port district on the way. Ask at the Tourist Information Centre (*see p33*) for details about boat trips.

Verdmanes Darvs

Until Napoleon rumbled towards Rīga in 1812 this green oasis was a residential district, but the Russians razed the houses to set up an artillery battery as part of their attempts to defend the city. Today this quiet retreat is the preserve of old men racking their chess brains, with a small theatre space that is sometimes used in summer.

The River Daugava with Rīga's Old Town in the background

The open-air Ethnographic Museum

OUTSIDE THE CENTRE

While there is plenty to keep visitors occupied in the Old Town and Art Nouveau quarters for days, it is worth going off the beaten track and spending an afternoon or two exploring this sprawling city beyond the obvious attractions of its historic core.

Bralu Kapi (Brethren Cemetery)

This memorial, a 4km (2½-mile) tram ride northeast of the Old Town, shows just how rapidly politics changed in this part of the world. What was intended as a post-World War I testament to local troops who had distinguished themselves fighting for Tsarist Russia soon became more synonymous with rising Latvian nationalism. The heroic sculptures of Karlis Zale stand proudly over neat rows of headstones with a certain sense of drama. Outside the main military cemetery are less ostentatious civilian graveyards set in pleasing woodland.
Berzu Iela. Free admission. Tram 11.

Latvijas Etnogrāfiskais Brīvības Muzejs (Latvian Ethnographic Museum)

Just 12km (7 miles) east of the Old Town is this impressive open-air display of traditional Latvian living. Set in attractive woodland, this re-creation of 19th-century Latvia needs a whole morning or afternoon to explore. Some of the timber buildings are originals that were shipped in from other parts of the country, while others were custom-built for the museum. On summer weekends when there are craft fairs the place can get packed, and in the run-up to Christmas there is a surge of Yuletide festivities. English guidebooks are available at the site at a nominal cost.
Brīvības Gatve 440. Tel: 6799 4515. Admission charge. Bus 1.

Rīgas Motormuzejs (Rīga Motor Museum)

At first glance, this bizarre museum, located 8km (5 miles) east of Rīga's Old Town, looks like a car showroom. Closer scrutiny reveals a collection of over 100 vehicles, including the former wheels of such renowned communist hardliners (less well known as car buffs) as the Russians Stalin, Khrushchev and Brezhnev, and the East German Erich Honecker. A nice touch is the wax figures, which create surreal sights such as the late Brezhnev sitting proudly in his Rolls-Royce or Stalin in his specially modified armoured car. Look out also for the old fire engine, which dates back to the start of the 20th century.

Eizenšteina Iela 6. Tel: 6709 7170. www.motormuzejs.lv. Admission charge. Bus 15 or 21.

Salaspils

About 18km (11 miles) southeast of Rīga lies the main legacy of Latvia's Nazi tragedy. Between 1941 and 1944, an estimated 100,000 innocents – including 55,000 Jews from Rīga – were murdered at a concentration camp at Salaspils. Today, the camp is preserved as a reminder of those dark days; there is also a small museum. The poignant inscription at the entrance reads, 'Behind this gate the earth groans.' The retreating Germans torched most of the evidence of their horrors and the main visual features today are

incongruous pieces of Soviet triumphalist sculpture that were erected at the site, also serving as a reminder of Latvia's 20th-century suffering. One stop away from Salaspils by train is the Rumbala forest where thousands were brutally murdered by Nazi forces.

Free admission. Suburban train to Darzini.

Soviet sculptures in Salaspils, once a Nazi concentration camp, now open as a memorial to all who died here

The beach at Jūrmala

JŪRMALA

Jūrmala in Latvian literally means coast, an apt name for Rīga's Baltic Sea playground to the west of the Lielupe River. This EU Blue Flag-winning 33km (21-mile) stretch of sweeping sands is awash with holidaying locals, an ever-increasing number of foreign tourists and buzzing music festivals in the summer. While things are quieter off-season, Jūrmala is renowned as a health and spa resort all the year round. Whatever the time of year, you can enjoy its charming wooden architecture – much of it now revamped after decades of Soviet-era neglect.

Beaches

The reason most Rīgans come to Jūrmala is for its beaches, and the award-winning stretch of sands is indeed impressive, especially when you consider that during the Soviet era there were serious problems of pollution. There is plenty of space here to find

your own hideaway, though the stretch around Majori can get uncomfortably crowded in summer – the upside is that you will find plenty of hotels, cafés and restaurants to cater to visitors.

Lielupe and Dzintari

A flurry of small towns and villages make up Jūrmala, all of them linked by road and many also by train. Lielupe, with some fine examples of Latvia's typical wooden architecture, lies farthest west. Dzintari is named after the amber that is still sometimes found on this coastline, and is worth visiting for its museums.
Museum of Prison History: 6–14 Piestātnes Iela. Tel: 2941 6038. Museum of Old Machinery: Turaidas Iela 11. Tel: 2926 3329.

Spas

All kinds of treatment are on offer in the famous spas here (*see pp50–1*). There are countless options to choose from. Some of the most tourist-friendly ones are listed below.

Alve Spa Hotel

This spa takes a holistic approach to health and wellbeing, offering teas and fruit juices designed to cleanse the liver and other vital organs alongside a host of pampering treatments. Steam baths, massages, body wraps and thalassotherapy are just some of the therapies that make the Alve Spa a great place to unwind.
Jomas Iela 88a, Majori. Tel: 6775 5970.

Amber Spa

Simple surrounds with a good range of treatments such as hydromassage, mud wraps, paraffin baths and a wide variety of massages.

Meza Prospekts 49, Bulduri.
Tel: 6775 5331. www.amberspa.lv

Aquae Triumphus

The spa centre at the TB Palace offers a wide range of beauty and pampering treatments, making it perfect for an indulgent short break. Manicures, pedicures, hairdressing, make-up application and waxing are all on offer, as are body wraps, aromatherapy massages, rejuvenating baths and thalassotherapy. After a day of pampering you can undo all the good work at the hotel's wine bar, which has a wide selection of wines from Austria and Alsace.

TB Palace Hotel & Spa, Pilsoņu Iela 8, Majori. Tel: 6714 7094.
www.tbpalace.com

Baltic Beach Hotel Spa Centre

A large hotel with a spot-on location overlooking the beach and an impressive range of treatments.

Juras Iela 23/25, Majori.
Tel: 6777 1400. www.balticbeach.lv

Hotel Jūrmala Spa

Opened in 2005, this excellent hotel and spa lays claim to being Jūrmala's best in both categories. The treatments include everything from hot stone therapy and Thai massage through to the more unusual salt room therapy and 'romantic bath for two'. The latter is a blissful experience starting with a cosy bath together and ending with a massage for two at the hands of two therapists.

Jomas Iela 47/49. Tel: 6778 4400.
www.hoteljurmala.com

Other activities

There is more to do in Jūrmala than just laze on the beach or relax in a spa. Plenty of adrenaline-pumping activities are on offer: apart from walks and jogs along the sands, it is possible to hire bikes, head out on horseback, get in a set or two of tennis and, of course, take to the Baltic Sea. Here you can sail, water ski, wakeboard and jet ski. A more controlled aquatic experience is provided by the **Līvu Akvaparks water park** (*see p153*).

BLUE FLAG BEACHES

Beaches and marinas in Europe are awarded Blue Flags according to strict criteria relating to both environmental management and water quality. In 2007 eight of Latvia's beaches were awarded Blue Flags: most on the coast at Liepāja and Ventspics, but also inland in Tukums and Daugaupils. For beach-goers this means that these beaches are free from industrial sewage, that the sands are clean, and that there are plenty of waste disposal facilities on hand, as well as public toilets. In the high season you may also find lifeguards on the beach. For more information about these beaches, check out the Blue Flag website: *www.blueflag.org*

Walk: Around Majori

Walking is a good way to explore Majori – the main settlement of Jūrmala – and with so many trees and the Baltic Sea breezes it is a health treatment in itself. The route is more or less flat and can be easily accomplished in a morning or an afternoon.

Distance: 3–3.5km (2–2¹/₄ miles). Time: allow 2 hours, or 4 hours including visits to the historic houses.

1 Tourist office

This is a good place to pick up free maps and information on what is going on locally, with friendly staff on hand to help you in the Jūrmala area.

From the tourist office turn left onto Tirgoņu Iela where you will find the city museum near the junction on the right-hand side.

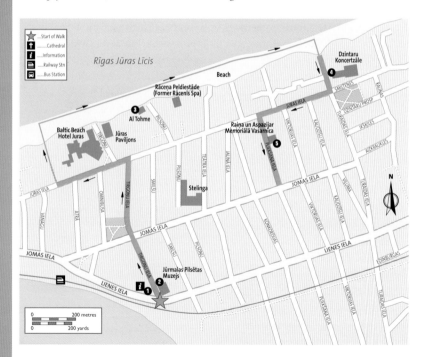

2 Jūrmalas Pilsētas Muzejs (Jūrmala City Museum)

This is an essential stop for anyone with more than a passing interest in the development of Jūrmala as a spa resort. The exhibits chart Jūrmala's highs and lows from the end of the 19th century, covering its heyday as an upmarket resort before World War I, right through to its recent renaissance. *From the museum follow Tirgoņu Iela north to Jūras Iela, and turn left. Take the next access path to the beach (on your right). Head right when you reach the beach.*

3 Al Tohme

The last thing you may expect to find on a Baltic beach is a Lebanese restaurant, but this soulful, relaxed venue with a view over the sands and sea is the perfect place to unwind, whether you just want a coffee on the terrace outside or are looking for a variety of mezze as fuel for the rest of your walk. *Stay on the beach, passing the former Rācenis Spa, until you reach Turaidas Iela and the Concert Hall*

4 Dzintaru Koncertzāle (Dzintaru Concert Hall)

This impressive concert hall enjoys a prime location right on the shore of the Baltic. Created by the architects Mellenbergs and Birzenieks, the building has been the pride of Majori's residents for over 70 years. It is at its best when a concert is being held on the outdoor summer stage.

Head south along Turaidas Iela and take the first road on the right, Jūras Iela. Follow the road until you reach Pliekšāna Iela (the third left) and the location of the next stop.

5 Raiņa un Aspazijas Memoriālā Vasarnīca (Rainis and Aspazija Summer House)

Jānis Rainis (*see p103 and p121*) and Aspazija (born Elza Rozenberga) were the leading literary lights of independent Latvia in the 1920s, and they spent a large part of their lives in Jūrmala. Their summer cottage is now open as a museum, which, through a collection of the couple's personal belongings and other artefacts, offers a real feel for their lives and times. This is also a good way to look around one of the gorgeous wooden houses for which Jūrmala is famous. *Head south along Pliekšāna Iela until you reach the central pedestrianised street Jomas Iela, whose cafés and bars are a pleasant place to relax after your walk.*

Tourist Office
Lienes Iela 5. Tel: 6714 7900. www.jurmala.lv
Jūrmala City Museum
Tirgoņu Iela 29. Tel: 6776 4746.
Admission charge.
Al Tohme
Pilsoņu 2. Tel: 6775 5755.
Dzintaru Concert Hall
Turaidas Iela 1. Tel: 6776 2092. www.dzk.lv
Rainis and Aspazija Summer House
Pliekšāna Iela 5/7. Tel: 6776 4295.
Admission charge.

Jūrmala spas

Jūrmala Spa Hotel

Latvia's coast has always offered perfect conditions for spa resorts. It is blessed with sweeping white sand beaches and soothing Baltic breezes that blow away the cobwebs, bountiful mineral-laden waters (mainly sulphur and bromide) and mud that is said to have medicinal qualities. Just strolling on the Blue Flag sands is soothing in itself.

The role of Jūrmala's 33km (21-mile) long coastal strip as a health spa resort dates back as far as 1838 when the Russian Tsar Nicholas II allowed the first bathing house using local mineral waters to open its doors. In 1870 Dr. Johann Christian Nordtsram became the man behind the first dedicated spa, Marienbade in Majori, using heat and mud treatment and bathing. The railways reached the region in 1877, boosting Jūrmala's popularity yet further. By World War I the region was booming with spas, many of them housed in elegant, wooden period buildings all along the coast. The founding of the first independent state of Latvia helped the boom continue through the 1920s and 1930s. European royalty and the continent's movers and shakers descended on the region looking for cures for their ailments and an escape from increasingly busy big-city lives.

The decadence of spa treatments in elegant surroundings did not sit easily with the ideals of the Soviet Union, but the communist years saw a boom of their own as mass health tourism grew in Jūrmala. The sick and convalescents from all over the Soviet Union came to Jūrmala to seek cures in the huge sanatoriums and health farms; by the 1980s around 300,000 visitors a year were flocking in, despite the increasing industrialisation and militarisation of the Latvian coast. The main cures were targeted at cardiac problems, neurology, and digestive and motor disorders.

With independence and the dissolution of the Soviet Union the main market for Jūrmala dried up almost overnight, and the area suffered an economic downturn. In recent years, though, a resurgence of interest across Europe in spa holidays has helped bring both visitors and investment to Jūrmala. There are now 50 spa facilities in the Jūrmala region, housed in both modern buildings and more characterful older structures. Many of the hotels, such as the Alve Spa Hotel, the Baltic Beach Hotel, the TB Palace Hotel and the

Hotel Jūrmala Spa, have spa facilities of their own (*see pp46–7*).

In the first half of 2005 there was a 30 per cent increase in the number of visitors to Jūrmala, a sure sign that the coastline which was once a top spa getaway is firmly on the way to rediscovering its golden days. The main clientele at present is from Sweden, followed by Estonia and Lithuania, though there are signs that the Russians are starting to come back and word is getting out in Western Europe too. A new development is the regeneration of the huge Ķemeri spa complex. The spa and the ultra-luxurious Kempinski Ķemeri Palace Resort will together make for one of Europe's largest spas, with myriad treatments including mud wraps, mineral baths and massages when it opens in 2009.

Saunas are an integral part of the Latvian spa experience

Kurzeme

The Kurzeme region covers the western flank of Latvia in a collage of thick forests, voluminous sand dunes and rumbling seas. From the Gulf of Riga right around the Livonian coast and down to the Lithuanian border, Kurzeme offers not only some of Latvia's most impressive scenery but some of the finest in Europe. Throw in two of Latvia's most vibrant, upcoming cities, Ventspils and Liepāja, and a sprinkling of other towns and villages that are well worth visiting.

History

Kurzeme, or the Duchy of Courland as it was once known to English speakers, boasts its own distinctive history. Strolling around the lazy dirt roads of its sleepy rural villages today, it is hard to imagine that this used to be a regional economic powerhouse. Courland once flourished as a major Baltic power that even had its own, albeit modest, overseas possessions in Africa and the Caribbean. By the 20th century, however, the region had fallen into decline, and although the Soviet use of the ports of Ventspils and Liepāja did create jobs it also damaged the environment that the locals have always held so dear. In the post-independence years Ventspils and Liepāja have enjoyed a boom as ice-free ports, with much of the incoming finance used wisely to revamp the cities and also to diversify into other sectors such as tourism.

Ķemeri National Park

Just west of Jūrmala, before setting out to enjoy the rest of the coast it is well worth stopping off at the Ķemeri National Park. This protected expanse of land is awash with bog and thick forests, though thankfully there are walking trails with duckboards at hand to keep you out of the wettest parts. The park was founded in 1997 and its facilities have been upgraded with a dedicated visitors' centre.

The land that Ķemeri lies on was once part of the Littorina Sea and today consists largely of sulphurous bog, which gives the local mineral water its distinctive taste. This mineral-rich water also helped to make the area popular as a spa escape with its centre at the formerly grand Ķemeri Palace Hotel. This building was recently bought by the Kempinski Group who are in the process of totally revamping it (*see p51*).

The bog-laden landscape of Ķemeri made for tough and trying terrain during World War I when fighting swept through the area; there are still signs of the old trenches.

Ķemeri is now something of an oasis for birds and ornithologists alike, as a centre on key migration routes. One of the most popular spots for birdwatching is the shallow Lake Kanieris. Among the myriad species are whitebacked woodpecker, geese, cranes and corncrakes, which share the park with deer, wild boar and even a type of insect-eating plant. Over 3,000 people still live within the boundaries of the park, some of them engaged in smoking fish, a delicious local delicacy. For more information about Ķemeri National Park, *see p136.*

Ķemeri National Park Visitor Information Centre, Meza Maja, Ķemeri. Tel: 6714 6819. www.kemeri.gov.lv

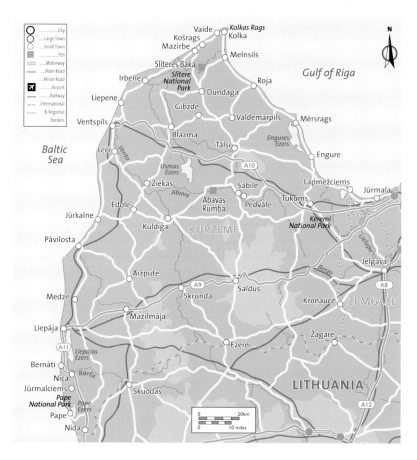

Latvian coastal scenery

Coast west of Jūrmala and Ķemeri

While Jūrmala grabs all the tourist headlines and pulls in the crowds, the coastline that stretches northwest from Jūrmala boasts plenty of attractions of its own. For much of its length it is blessed with perfect white sand beaches backed by tall pine trees, and there is little of the tourism development you will find back in Jūrmala. There are some parking places equipped with toilets and picnic benches just off the main coastal road (they also offer secure parking for a small fee during the summer), and if you are looking for

total serenity there is plenty of space to find your own private spot. Early autumn is a particularly pleasant time to visit as you will have what seems like the whole coast to yourself without the cold of the winter.

Engures Ezers (Lake Engure)

This inland lake with the same name as a small village, just a short drive from the main coastal road, stretches for around 20km (12 miles) and is often as much as 4km (2½ miles) wide, making it the country's third-largest lake. Engure is something of a mecca for ornithologists, but the facilities are pretty rudimentary so if you are in a hurry it may be best to stop off and take in the view from the observation tower – though you should call ahead to make sure it is open. Spring and autumn are the ideal times to visit, when masses of migratory birdlife can be enjoyed in this unspoilt area. The flora is impressive too, with 22 types of orchids recorded. The 'Orchid Trail' is a 3.5km (2¼-mile) walk that edges the park. If you have a serious interest in the park, the park authorities can put you in touch with a professional guide. For more information about Lake Engure *see p137*.

Lapmežciems

If you like smoked fish, this is the place to be. Traditionally the local catch was preserved by smoking so that the people could make it through the tough winter months when the boats could not go out to net fresh fish. The smoking of fish then developed into quite an art and today Rīgans can often be seen coming out to Lapmežciems at weekends to pick up the excellent local produce. You would be well advised to follow suit by buying direct or tasting the local fare in one of the informal eateries.

Mērsrags

This fishing town may not be the prettiest place on the Latvian coast, but is worth a brief stop to see its modest museum, lighthouse and the Lutheran church.

Mērsrags Tourist Information Centre, Dzintaru Iela 1/9. Tel: 6323 5470. www.mersrags.lv

Roja

Roja is a well-established fishing village that makes few concessions to tourism, but is worth stopping off at either to enjoy a coffee or something more substantial at the excellent Roja Hotel. You can sample the fresh catch of local fishermen whose boats you can see moored at the northern outskirts of the village. Fishing here is back in local hands after attempts by Moscow to collectivise it, and you can delve into these events at the local Fishing Museum.

Roja Tourist Information Centre, Selgas Iela 33. Tel: 6326 9594. www.roja.lv

Beach on the Gulf of Rīga

Amber – Latvian gold

On first sighting *dzintars* (amber) in a souvenir shop in Rīga, one may wonder what all the fuss is about. This slightly dull precious stone may not have the immediate striking effect, of say, a diamond, but it was once so vital to the region that the local people along the coast were banned by the Teutonic Knights from collecting it on pain of death – a ban that was not lifted until the 19th century. The Latvian people often refer to the Baltic Sea as the 'Amber Sea' and both local men and women are named after amber (*Dzintars* for males and *Dzintra* for females); many hotels, shops and restaurants also have similarly amber-themed names.

In days gone by, as the region became part of larger trade routes across Europe, local tribes used amber to trade with the Romans. The widespread value of amber is demonstrated by the discovery of amber in Egyptian tombs that were sealed as long ago as the 4th millennium BC; there is also evidence in present-day Latvia of

Amber products geared towards tourists

amber artefacts that date from this period. At one time amber was as valued in parts of Europe as gold.

The discovery of amber is shrouded in local legends. Some say that it was a gift of the gods that inhabit the depths of the Baltic Sea, though the reality is a little more prosaic: Latvia's amber comes from the resin that oozed out of pine trees and then fossilised in the Baltic Sea region around 30–40 million years ago.

Amber is found in various parts of the world, as far afield as Japan and Alaska, but the largest quantities, and the variety that many connoisseurs reckon has the highest quality, come from the Baltic Sea. Normally the stone appears a clear amber colour, but it can also be found with insects trapped within it or pine needles embedded within. Amber is washed up in small amounts on the coasts of all the three Baltic Republics, especially after raging storms, when hopeful locals can be seen trawling the sands in search of fragments of the Latvian gold.

In Latvia, and especially Rīga, an increasing number of souvenir shops are specialising in amber, which, compared to many other precious stones, is easy to shape. It comes in the form of necklaces, bracelets, earrings, as beads and, perhaps most strikingly, as a single brooch.

Amber necklace; amber jewellery is a very popular souvenir

The tricky part of buying amber is not choosing the piece of jewellery that most catches your eye but making sure that what you are buying is genuine. This can be tricky especially at impromptu market stalls; buying in a recognised amber shop is usually a safer option. When you are back home admiring your Baltic amber, spare a thought for amber's other uses. This versatile stone compound is composed mainly of succinic acid (99.8 per cent), which is reputed to have medicinal qualities, and is also used in such niche markets as in the making of nuclear submarines and spacecraft engines.

Kurzeme interior

While it is the coast that attracts most visitors to the Kurzeme region, the quiet inland byways of this unspoilt part of the country also have much to offer: charming towns and villages and plenty of opportunity for travelling across the picturesque landscape.

Tukums

Those with a penchant for culture may want to break their journey to Kurzeme with a detour to Tukums. Here you can explore the **Livonijas Ordeņa Pils** (Livonian Order Castle) (*Brīvibās Laukums 19a*) which opens up the history of today's rather modest town. It is an interesting tour as most of the other Livonian remnants in the region are in ruin. Also worth checking out on the outskirts of town are the **Jaunmoku Pils** (Jaunmoku Palace) and the **Durbes Pils** (Durbe Castle) (*Mazā Parka Iela 7*), the former housing a modest forestry museum in a building partly owned by the Latvian Forestry Authority, and the latter a 17th-century palace now open as a museum delving into Latvian rural life with pleasant grounds. Tukums is also home to a trio of interesting churches: a Lutheran one (*Brīvibās Laukums 1*), a Catholic one (*Harmonijas Iela 1a*) and an Orthodox one (*Pils Iela 13*). The town's beach has recently been awarded Blue Flag status by the EU.
Tukums Tourist Information Centre, Pils Iela 3. Tel: 6312 4451. www.tukums.lv

Talsi

This impressive little town epitomises the Kurzeme interior. There is no one thing to put your finger on, but the combination of a sleepy lake, a ramble of waterfront houses, cobbled streets

Homes on the lake's edge in Talsi

Dundaga's manor house beside the lake

and a grassy mound where a grand castle once stood make for a pleasant day trip or lunch stop. Liejā Iela is where the majority of the town's life flourishes, but for the best view of Talsi stop at the Lutheran church on the hillside that has recently been refurbished and follow the grassy track up to where a Livonian Order castle once proudly overlooked the town. A castle stood on the site in the 12th century as evidenced by the English and German coins from that period that were uncovered by archaeologists. As you enjoy the view, also note to the left of the town a striking stone memorial to local rebels who held out for decades against the Russians after Latvia was occupied at the end of World War II.

Talsi Tourist Information Centre, Liēla Iela 19-21. Tel: 322 4165. www.talsi.lv

Dundaga

Dundaga is one of the few towns in the world, and certainly the only one in Latvia, famous for its crocodiles – given to the city by the Latvian Consulate in Chicago to mark an eminent citizen who emigrated to Australia. Arvīds Blūmentāls is said to have been the original 'Crocodile Dundee' of Hollywood fame. Dundaga is also home to a Lutheran church and a pleasant manor house that overlooks the town's lake.

Dundaga Tourist Information Centre, Pils Iela 14. Tel: 6323 2293. www.dundaga.lv

Sabile

This quiet town on the banks of the Abava River is the unlikely home of Europe's northernmost vineyard. Wine has been produced here since at least

The Pedvāle Sculpture Park boasts an eclectic array of weird and often wonderful exhibits

the 17th century, although production is very much on a small scale. You can taste a glass or two locally, though you will hardly ever see a bottle outside of the town. Elsewhere in Sabile there is a Lutheran church as well as an old synagogue that is now home to temporary cultural exhibitions. *Sabile Tourist Information Centre, Pilskalna Iela 6. Tel: 6325 2344. www.sabile.lv*

Pedvāle

If you enjoy the outdoors and like sculpture, then the Pedvāle Sculpture Park is just for you. Here, spread across 2sq km (³/₄sq mile), are several eclectic modern art creations linked by a network of walking trails. The countryside itself is charming, with plenty of greenery, stretches of forest and rushing streams. Pedvāle was the brainchild of Latvian sculptor Ojārs Feldbergs, who set it up in 1990; many of the works on display are his own. You can spend time here walking around the hilly park stepping through sculptures and taking in the rolling countryside as you go. Although some of the installations may not be exactly award winners, children and adults alike love this park. If there is a school group visiting you may be well advised to rest in the friendly bar/restaurant at the entrance before braving the park. Make sure to ask for the English translations of the works that the staff lend out for free at the information centre, which is housed in the old Pedvāle Manor. *www.pedvale.lv*

Abavas Rumba (Abava Waterfall)

Within easy driving distance of Pedvāle is the Abavas Rumba (Abava Waterfall), which may not be as famous as Kuldīga's falls but is worth stopping for. It is said to be the second-widest waterfall in the country, at around 30m (100ft). A short stroll from the road brings you to Abava where the eponymous river drops down its aquatic steps (from anything between 0.5m/1¹/₂ft in summer to 2m/6¹/₂ft in winter) in a camera-pleasing rush with a phalanx of tall trees framing the scene.

Aizpute

Tourism has yet to really hit Aizpute, and this laid-back town (whose first written mention dates back as far as 1378) is all the better for it. While there may not be enough cafés, bars and restaurants to please tour-bus crowds, this leaves the quiet streets free for you to explore. The wooden houses around the lake have yet to be touched up and turned into holiday homes, giving the pleasing impression that even the 20th century, let alone the 21st, is yet to dawn in Aizpute. The only real 'sight' in town is the remains of a Knights of the Sword Castle.

Aizpute Tourist Information Centre,
Skolas Iela. Tel: 6344 8880.
www.aizpute.lv

Skrunda

Anyone wanting to slip back to the days of the Cold War should make a stop at Skrunda. This used to be an early warning station where the Soviets awaited a nuclear attack from the West that never came.

Although Latvia achieved independence in 1991 and some of the installation was ceremoniously destroyed in 1995, it was not until 1999 that the last of the Soviet troops finally left the site after Moscow's demand for an extension was rejected by Rīga. Today it stands as a ghostly Cold War dinosaur, though plans have been mooted to turn it into a leisure complex complete with houses, restaurants and bars. It is now also the venue for a big annual rock and pop festival. *www.skrunda.lv*

Kurzeme countryside

Drive: The Livonian coast

The Livonian coast, the epic land where the ethnic Livs once held sway but today are forced to cling on to their existence (see pp16–17), is a spectacular area to drive around. Be sure to take a decent car, though, as many of the roads are unsurfaced, with some of the coastal tracks little more than compacted sand dunes. The following route sticks to the best roads but care should still be taken, especially in inclement weather, as this is no tourist theme park but a beautiful and wild escape.

Distance: 30km (19 miles). Time: allow 5–6 hours with stops.

From Jūrmala, follow the coastal road (P128, later becoming P131) via Engure, and Roja until you reach Kolka.

1 Kolka

This modest village is a pleasant little place with wooden houses set back from the worst ravages of the Baltic. There is not much to see, but it offers a good base for those looking to stay in the area.

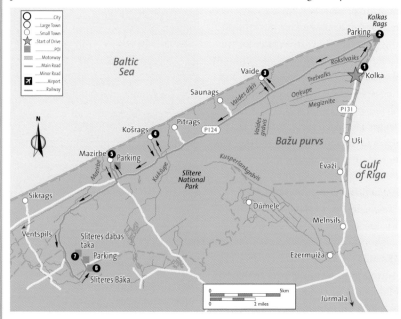

www.kolka.lv
Head north on the P131 for
approximately 3km (2 miles).

2 Kolkas Rags (Cape Kolka)

This wild spot is where the Gulf of Rīga clashes with the Baltic Sea. It is a dangerous stretch of coastline; swimming is a definite no-no. There are a number of walking trails allowing you to walk back towards Kolka.
Drive southwest on P124, then follow the sign to Vaide. Allow 15 minutes.

3 Vaide

The unassuming old Livonian village of Vaide is home to the unusual *Ragu Kolekcija* (Horn Collection). You can easily spot it by the antlers above the entrance. Opening hours vary.
Retrace your route back to the road P124 and head southwest to Košrags. Allow 20–30 minutes.

4 Košrags

This is a quaint little fishermen's village, spread out amongst the dunes.
Return once again to the main P124, head southwest and keep your eyes peeled for signs to Mazirbe. Allow 20 minutes.

5 Mazirbe

Mazirbe is one of the most important villages on this stretch of the coastline as it houses the Libiešu Tautas Nams (Livonian Cultural Centre). Exhibitions and cultural events are a regular feature; outside is a striking wooden memorial to Liv culture.

The colourful Slītere Lighthouse offers sweeping views

Back on the P124, travel southwest for 3km (2 miles) then due south for another 3km (2 miles). Keep your eyes peeled for the brown tourist sign to Slītere Lighthouse. Allow 20–30 minutes.

6 Slīteres Baka (Slītere Lighthouse)

This striking red lighthouse rises not, as you may expect, by the Baltic coastline, but a few kilometres inshore. You can climb to the top for a small fee and enjoy sweeping views over the seemingly endless Livonian forests and out towards the Baltic.
Don a pair of walking shoes and head for the nature trail behind the lighthouse.

7 Slītere National Park Trail

Officially you have to ask at Slītere Lighthouse and pay for a guide to lead you down the nature trail that breaks away to the east; however, you can also embark on the walk yourself.
Follow the coast road (P124) south to Ventspils where there is plenty of accommodation. Allow 1–1½ hours.

Kuldīga

Kuldīga lays a fair claim to being the most attractive town in Latvia – a chocolate-box beauty of winding streets, old wooden houses and waterways, as well as being home to what locals claim to be Europe's widest waterfall. This inland oasis is also regarded as one of the most authentic Latvian towns as it never suffered Russification; its population still remains over 90 per cent ethnic Latvian.

Kuldīga was founded in the 13th century and its golden age came a hundred years later when it was a proud and prosperous member of the Hanseatic League. This strategic town was valued by everyone from the rampaging Vikings and crusading German Knights through to marauding Swedish kings who breezed through the town over the centuries. At the height of the Hanseatic League the Venta River buzzed with life as the town's ships ventured as far as the Duchy of Courland's colonies in Africa and the Caribbean; things are very different in sleepy Kuldīga these days.

Kuldīga Tourist Information Centre, Baznīcas Iela 5. Tel: 6332 2259. www.kuldiga.lv

Old Town

Kuldīga's Old Town, outside the protective walls of Kuldīga's castle, is one of the most charming in the Baltics. It may not quite be the 'Latvian Venice' of the tourist brochures, but the 17th- and 18th-century wooden houses that huddle around the Alekšupīte River make it a perfect venue for idle strolls. You can delve through nooks and crannies and old alleys, and watch the river gurgling through; the scene is framed by a necklace of green spaces. The heart of the old town, Baznīcas Iela, is based around the refurbished Rātslaukums (Old Town Hall), reputedly the oldest building in Kuldīga (dating back to 1670). This is a good place to start and finish your walk as there is an excellent tourist office located here. There are also a sprinkling of cafés and restaurants around the square. In Baznīcas Iela, look out for the building at No 8, the only one left

Avant-garde sculpture in a park in Kuldīga

Narrow passageway in Kuldīga Old Town

standing in the attractive and very distinctive German half-timbered Fachwerk style.

Kuldīga churches

Kuldīga boasts a number of interesting churches catering to all strands of the local population. The Catholic Svētā Katrīnas Baznīca (St Catherine's Church) was the first church to open (completed in 1640), and the legendary Duke Jakob of Courland was baptised here. Look out for the coat of arms of Kuldīga above the side entrance and the baroque wooden altar. The highlight of another Catholic place of worship, the starch-white Svētā Trīsvienības Baznīca (Church of the Holy Trinity), is its lavish 19th-century altar (apparently a gift from Tsar Alexander I). Also interesting is the *Madonna and Child* which was painted in the 14th century. Kuldīga's Lutheran church was completed in 1904, while the Russian Orthodox church,

housed within a pleasant little park and with distinctive onion domes, dates from the 19th century.

Kuldīga District Court

This impressive 19th-century building stands near where the Livonian castle complex once presided over the town. Used by both the Soviets and the Germans during the 20th century, it now functions as the court for Kuldīga and the surrounding region. It was recently refurbished.

Kuldīgas Muzejs (Kuldīga Museum)

This museum, near the site where Kuldīga's grand castle once stood on the Venta River, opens up the history of not only Kuldīga but also that of the surrounding region. The museum building itself is interesting as it was shipped in from Paris where it was part of the 'Russian' section of a world exposition. A wealthy Kuldīga resident decided to impress his beloved, bought the impressive wooden building and brought it to Kuldīga in 1900; it became a museum in 1940. A highlight of the 85,000-strong collection is the old black-and-white images of the town, recounting its development from the 19th century onward. Sculptures by local artist Līvija Rezevskas can be seen in the park that separates the museum from the old town. If you are impressed with the sculptures, you can seek out Rezevskas' studio (*Mucenieku 19*), which was opened to the public in 2003.
Pils Iela 5. Tel: 6335 0179.

Traditional wooden architecture at the Kuldīga Museum

Venta Bridge

The red-brick bridge over the Venta makes for a dramatic sight, a grand crossing that seems slightly incongruous in the relaxed Kuldīga of today. It was built in 1874 to allow horse carriages to pass and is one of the largest of its kind left standing in Europe. Destroyed in 1915, it was painstakingly rebuilt in 1926.

Ventas Rumba (Venta Waterfall)

The Venta has always been key to the fortunes of Kuldīga. The town was almost destroyed in a massive flood in 1615. On the plus side, the Ventas Rumba prevents shipping from going further upstream, making Kuldīga the terminus for river journeys. The Ventas Rumba is perhaps the town's most famous attraction; the citizens of Kuldīga recently brought in independent assessors to confirm that, at 250m (820ft), it is the widest waterfall in Europe. It may have a drop of only around 2m (6¹/₂ft), but after heavy rain it is an impressive mist-shrouded sight. The Venta is renowned for its rich salmon runs, and local tour guides tell tales of fishermen who once hung out holding baskets at the fall in an effort to catch the leaping salmon. In summer the shallow waters around the falls are a popular spot for swimming and relaxing.

Around Kuldīga

Adventure sports lovers will find plenty to keep them occupied in the Kuldīga region. The local tourist office can help you organise everything from genteel fishing trips, horse riding, boat trips or cycling right through to hunting, paintballing, snowmobiling, water skiing and 4×4 driving. The 'Soviet Charm Show' is a surreal experience where you can drive around in old Soviet-era cars, try retro food and even get married 'Soviet-style'. For details, ask at the local tourist office.

Kurzeme

Venta Waterfall, the widest in Europe

Ventspils

The city of Ventspils is a wealthy and prosperous place, a booming oil town, which may come as something of a surprise as Latvia itself does not produce oil. Instead, over ten per cent of Russia's crude oil ships stop at Ventspils on their route to the Western European markets, helping to make Ventspils the country's busiest port.

Trade has always been crucial to Ventspils. For a couple of centuries it was a member of the Hanseatic League, but after World War II it fell into decline as the Soviet military took over the region. The dynamic mayor Aviars Lembergs is the man behind the current revival of the port's trade (much of it transshipments from and to other countries). Ventspils' port is now the largest hub in the world for the transshipment of potassium salt.

Lembergs is also credited with the recent reinvention of the city as the country's most popular day-trip destination for Latvians, with a revamped city centre, an array of public sculptures and an attractive beach that has gone from being one of the Baltic's most polluted beaches to an EU Blue Flag winner in an impressively short period of time.

Clearly, Lembergs had seen the writing on the wall for the future of the oil industry and he was proved right in 2005 when Germany and Russia signed a massive deal to sideline Latvia and pump oil direct through a pipeline under the Baltic. Tourism may soon become the biggest business in Ventspils and the city is getting ready for it.

Ventspils Tourist Information Centre, Tirgus Iela 7. Tel: 6362 2263. www.ventspils.lv

Akvaparks Ventspils (Aqua Park Ventspils)

Situated just behind the Ventspils Blue Flag beach and near the Open-Air Museum, this is a perfect place to let your hair down. The orgy of slides and pools make it one of the city's most popular attractions. The revamped Aqua Park (which now has a 10m/33ft water tower to accompany the 8m/26ft one) is part of a larger sports complex that also boasts a skate park, tennis courts, ice-skating rink and athletics track.

Mendu Iela 19. Tel: 6366 5853. www.ocventspils.lv. Open: May–Sept. Admission charge.

THE HANSEATIC LEAGUE

The Hanseatic League was a sort of proto-European Union. This pan-Baltic trading and economic association boasted members from all over the Baltic Sea region, at one point numbering over 150. It was a loose organisation based upon the principle of collective bargaining, with various cities coming together to negotiate collectively with the likes of England and the Low Countries. The golden age of the Hanseatic League was in the 14th century, but it continued to exist until as late as 1669 when the last grand assembly was staged. The Latvian members included Rīga, Cēsis and Kuldīga.

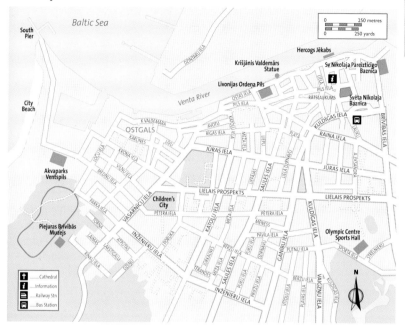

Ventspils

Beaches

Reinvention of the once-polluted sands was completed in 1999 when they were awarded EU Blue Flag status. There are finer (and quieter) beaches both north and south of the city, but if you are in town on a hot day the city beach is a pleasant place to relax for an afternoon. In summer it is very popular with families. You can also walk from the beach all the way north to the mouth of the Venta River and watch the ships cruise in and out of the busy port.

Churches

Ventspils is home to an array of attractive churches. The Lutheran Church on Tirgus Iela (*see p70*) was built in the 19th century on the orders of Tsar Nicholas, while the Russian Orthodox Church on Plosta Iela (Svēta Nikolaja Pareizticīgo Baznīca) was opened at the start of the 20th century. Look out for the image of the Tsar inside. The church is topped with distinctive Orthodox onion domes.

Hercogs Jēkabs

This chunky little boat cruises the River Venta from its mooring on Ostas Iela. It explores the hulking port facilities, but is not as dull an experience as it sounds. It is a good way of getting an idea of the scale of the city as well as seeing it from a unique perspective.

Tel: 2635 3344. Open: May–Oct. Tickets available on the day, no advance booking. Tours last 45 minutes, subject to weather conditions. Tickets can be purchased from 9am by berth 18 on the day of travel.

Livonijas Ordeņa Pils (Livonian Order Castle)

One of the most impressive of Ventspils' recent achievements is this rebuilt castle, which reopened in 2001 at the site of the 13th-century original. Its history is somewhat chequered, having served as a prison under Tsarist Russia. The rather plain exterior belies an interior packed with well-presented audio-visual exhibits. The 'Living History' images illuminate the history of both the castle and the city.

Telescopes are available to take in views of the city. The castle also hosts a string of cultural events.
*Jana 17. Tel: 6362 2031.
www.ventspilsmuzejs.lv*

Old Town

The hub of the Old Town is Rātslaukums (Town Hall Square), which is now back to its 19th-century best. The most attractive building here is the striking Lutheran Svētā Nikolaja Baznīca (St Nicholas Church), which looms large over the square. Every month one more of the Old Town's buildings seems to rise from the ashes and the heart of the area is becoming an increasingly pleasant place to stroll around. So make sure to break away from the main square

Livonian Order Castle, a striking sight in Ventspils' old quarter

The boat *Hercogs Jēkabs* offers cruises on the River Venta

and head west to explore the old avenues with their collage of 18th- and 19th-century architecture. Before you reach the city's beaches you will pass the Ostgals district with its network of small wooden houses, which feels more like a coastal village than one of the country's most vibrant cities.

Ostas Iela
This waterfront promenade drifts by the fringes of the old town with the structures of the city's huge port dwarfing the view on one flank. As elsewhere in the city, there are a number of public sculptures: one of the most popular of these is a spouting fountain; the most famous ones are the string of seven 'Ventspils' cows that were erected in 2002; and a thematic one is a cow split in two by a section of an oil pipe. Look out also for the rather downcast figure of Krišjānis Valdemārs, erected in 2000 to commemorate the man credited with inventing Latvian shipping.

Piejuras Brīvibās Muzejs
(Seaside Open Air Museum)
This is a great place for children and adults alike. In summer a narrow-gauge train (built just after World War I) takes visitors around its environs, and cultural events are held here at weekends. The buildings that make up the museum explore the region's history through old cottages and a display of boats from different periods.
Riņķu Iela 2. Tel: 6362 4467.

Liepāja

The city of Liepāja, Latvia's third largest, is the other of Kurzeme's twin ice-free ports. It has always been a big rival of nearby Ventspils although it has not benefited to the same degree from the Russian oil trade. Liepāja has made a big effort in recent years to attract tourists from home and abroad, something it should be able to achieve without too much trying, given its lovely city beaches, the faded grandeur of its brick-and-wood 18th- and 19th-century architecture, and its lively nightlife.

The city centre is struggling to keep up with the pace of change led by the strident ambition of the authorities. While a number of buildings has been renovated and many shops, cafés and restaurants have been developed, many buildings still lie awaiting renovation after decades of Soviet-era neglect. The various layers of Liepāja's past, including its days as a Livonian Order stronghold, are gradually being restored to their best as investment flows in.

Liepāja Tourist Information Centre, Rožu Laukums 5/6. Tel: 6348 0808. www.liepaja.lv

Beaches

Liepāja's beaches have been cleaned up after years of being polluted by the surrounding heavy industrial units. The improvement has been recognised by the EU, who have awarded them the

Impressive architecture on the streets of Liepāja

coveted Blue Flag. Today they are one of the city's biggest draws, especially in summer.

Jūrmalas Parks (Seaside Park)

Set just to the west of the city centre is this well laid-out green space where you can take a stroll, relax on a bench or walk on towards the coast where Liepāja's sandy beaches await. Within the park there are some old spa buildings that date from the times when people flocked to the city in search of curative mud treatments. Like the rest of the city, these remnants of the past are slowly being renovated.

Karosta

Karosta has witnessed a dramatic turnaround, from being a major Warsaw Pact naval base, complete with thousands of Russian service personnel and a submarine fleet intent on thwarting the nuclear threat of the West, to now serving as a Latvian base with NATO troops that is no longer shut off to foreigners, let alone Latvians, but also actively encourages tourists. The 'Behind the Bars' tour of **Karosta prison** (*Invalīdu Iela 4*) is a throwback to the past where you are led by Latvians dressed in Russian uniforms and ushered in at gunpoint into old Soviet prison cells. You can even stay in one of these old KGB cells, be subjected to a prison regime of verbal abuse and be sleep-deprived throughout the night, a routine that is surprisingly popular amongst

Alexander Nevsky Church (*see p75*)

Latvians. You can book the tour at Liepāja tourist office.

The other main attraction in Karosta is the Orthodox **Svētā Nikolaja Katedrāle** (Church of St Nicholas) at Katedrāles 7. This beautiful onion-domed place of worship is an incongruity amongst the concrete apartment blocks littered all around, but somehow they only add to its appeal. Idling here on a Sunday, you can see the Orthodox population of Karosta come to hang on to all they have left now that the Russian military has gone.

Walk: Liepāja Old Town

Liepāja's pancake-flat Old Town invites walking. The tour takes in most of the main sights, but the city is changing rapidly so keep an eye out for new attractions and renovated buildings. Also take time to study the magnificent wooden houses that populate the city, which hark back to Liepāja's former grandeur.

Allow 1 hour, or 3 hours if you want to explore in detail the museum, the churches and the market.

Start your walk at Liepāja Museum on Kūrmājas prospekts.

1 Vēstures un Mākslas Muzejs (Liepāja Museum)

For all you want to know about the city, this is the place to start.
Kūrmājas prospekts 16–18. Tel: 6342 2973. www.liepajasmuzejs.lv. Admission charge.
Head east along Kūrmājas prospekts until you reach the junction with Lielā Iela. Turn right and follow the road for 250m (275yds).

2 Svētā Trīsvienības Baznīca (Church of the Holy Trinity)

The drab exterior of this large 18th-century structure may tempt you to simply walk past it. However, the Lutheran church has an impressive rococo interior complete with intricate carvings. The church is particularly atmospheric on Saturday afternoons in summer when organ recitals can be heard in full flow. Climb the tower and

you will be rewarded with sweeping views of the city.
Liēla Iela 9. Free admission.
Facing southeast on Baznīcas Iela turn right onto Stendera and head south until you reach Kungu Iela. Head east along Kungu Iela for 200m (220yds).

3 Pētera I Namiņš (Peter the Great's House)

This was where the Russian Tsar stayed when he was in town in 1697.
Kungu Iela 24.
Retrace your steps to the junction of Kungu Iela and Siea Iela and head southwest for 200m (220yds).

4 Svētā Annas Baznīca (St Anne's Church)

This Lutheran church was consecrated at the end of the 19th century. The neo-Gothic exterior may not grab your attention, but delve into the interior to discover the magnificent baroque altar sculpted by Nicolai Soffrens under Duke Jakob.

Eduarda Veidenbauma 1. Free admission. Looking west from the church you will see Peter's Market.

5 Pētertirgus (Peter's Market)

This old-school market offers a fascinating insight into the shopping world of pre-1991 Latvia. The bustling stalls and colourful sellers are a far cry from the hegemony of the supermarkets rapidly spreading across the country. Close to the main entrance you will also find a stall selling tasty organic honey.

Kuršu Laukums 5.
Exit the market onto Kuršu Laukums. Walk north for 150m (165yds), turn left onto Peldu Iela and walk 200m (220yds) west to the Cathedral of St Joseph.

6 Svētā Jāzepa Katedrāle (Cathedral of St. Joseph)

Completed at the turn of the 20th century, this is the Old Town's most attractive place of worship, both externally and internally.

K. Valdermasa 28.
Return to Peldu Iela and head west to the junction with Ūliha Iela. Turn left and walk 75m (80yds).

7 Aleksandra Nevska Baznīca (Alexander Nevsky Church)

Its gaudy colour scheme makes this small Orthodox church hard to miss. The church gate is often locked, so thrust your camera through the railings to get a good shot.

Ūliha Iela.

Walk: Liepāja Old Town

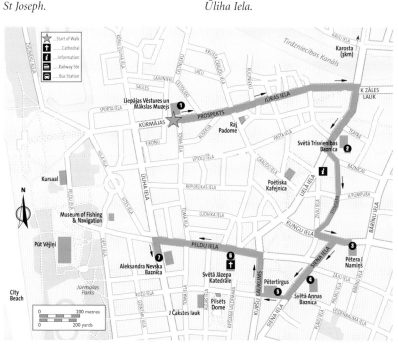

Coast south of Liepāja

Jūrmalciems

The Jūrmalciems turn-off on the A11 from Liepāja leads to two natural attractions. The first is Pusēns Hill, where you will find the highest sand dune on the entire Latvian littoral. A short distance to the south is Zalais Stars (Green Ray), the westernmost point in Latvia. Both are must-sees for the 'been there, done that' crowd. Besides, the scenery is spectacular on this stretch of the coastline.

Liepājas Ezers (Liepāja Lake)

Just south of Liepāja and accessible by bus or bike is the city's lake. A ramble of trails leads around the banks, making this a good getaway option if you are staying a few nights in the city.

If you are only passing through, it may be better to continue south where greater treasures await.

Nida

Literally on the Lithuanian border, Nida is the last turn-off on the A11. A dirt track leads from the border station (you don't have to actually cross over) 4km (2½ miles) out to the village of Nida, a windswept place submerged in sand dunes. You can park here and stroll on the sands, taking in the breeze that helps power the turbines in southern Kurzeme as you stare out to the sea and Lithuania.

Pape National Park and Lake Pape

There are two ways of seeing the Pape National Park (*see p138*), a park partly

The rich wetlands of the Pape National Park are alive with wildlife

The famous wild horses of Pape have recently made a comeback

financed by the World Wide Fund for Nature – the ubiquitous WWF panda symbol can be seen all over this part of Latvia. If you just want an overall view of the park and its birdlife (spring is the best time for keen ornithologists), head for the village of Pape. Just before the village, you can climb a wooden bird-watching tower on the right of the road and survey the landscape; you may want to check first at Liepāja, though, as it is sometimes closed out of season. Although this will give you a rough idea of the lie of the land, the chances are that you will not get to see any of Pape's famous wild horses.

Back up the A11 another turn-off leads to the small village of Kalniški. Here there is a hut where rangers will charge you a nominal fee to be led out in search of the horses. Centuries ago they used to roam free amidst the sand dunes and scrub, but human beings put paid to their reign. In the 1990s a local initiative with the backing of the WWF introduced semi-wild Polish horses into 150 hectares (370 acres) of land where they would be protected and allowed to roam and graze on the land. By 2006 there were 30 horses who were breeding well. If the trek to see the horses has not exhausted you, there is a 1km (2/3-mile) walk to the lake itself from behind the ranger's hut. Also look out for migratory birds and aurochs (European bison), or 'wild cows', as the rangers call them. There were around 30 aurochs in Pape in 2007.
www.pdf-pape.lv

The Zemgale region

The history and culture of the Zemgale region in the centre of Latvia, south of Rīga, are similar to that of other Latvian regions in that they were dominated by the peoples and countries around them, from the German crusaders right through to the Russians, all of whom have left their traces. Zemgale's lifeblood is the River Lielupe, which flows into the Gulf of Rīga near Jūrmala. It is a prosperous region where farming and manufacturing take centre stage, with tourism becoming increasingly important.

Zemgale is a region worth visiting for its three landmark palaces, Rundāle, Mežotne and Jelgava, and for its urban centres and nature parks.

Jelgava

Zemgale's largest city enjoyed its golden age between the 16th and 18th centuries when it was the capital of the Duchy of Courland, a prosperous empire that once stretched across the Baltic as far as Tobago and Africa. The 20th century was not very kind to the city, as the two World Wars damaged much of its architecture, but in the 21st century the city is making a comeback. *Jelgava Regional Tourist Information Centre, J. Čakstes Bulvāris 7. Tel: 6302 3874. www.jelgava.lv*

Jelgava Palace

The key attraction of the city is Jelgava Palace, a beautiful epic structure that is every bit as impressive as its more famous neighbour Rundāle Palace (*see pp84–5*), though it does not get anywhere near the number of tourists the latter does, perhaps because it is still used by the Latvian Agricultural College. Built on the

The striking Jelgava Palace is Jelgava's highlight

Zemgale

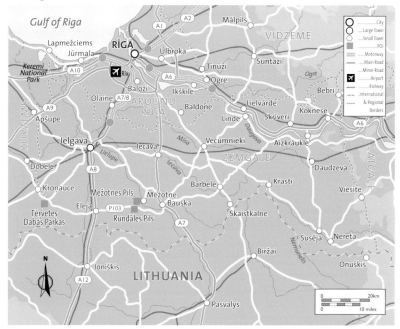

site of an old Livonian castle, Jelgava was commissioned by the same man behind Rundāle, Ernst Johann von Biron, the Duke of Courland. He employed the services of renowned architect Francesco Bartolomeo Rastrelli, who completed it by 1772. The palace has had a string of illustrious guests, ranging from French kings to members of the Russian royal family – it is said to have been one of the latter's favourites.

Today the palace bears a functional air inside, thanks to its educational role, but there is a small museum (opened in 1968) at hand to give you an idea of what it once looked like. The museum displays some of the exhibits unearthed by excavations at the site. If the staff are

in a good mood they may let you enter the inner sanctum in the basement of the eastern wing where the Dukes of Courland are buried. The resting place of Ernst Johann von Biron, of course, has the most ostentatious gravestone. One grotesque local story has it that when the Bolshevik Russian forces raided the tomb they riddled the corpses with bullets.

The palace's façade is still as grand as ever, enjoying a prime location right on the river. If you do not have the time for a visit, make sure to at least get a look as you head in or out of town on the Rīga road.

Lielā Iela 2. Tel: 300 5617.

Book in advance for guided tours.

Walk: Jelgava tour

This walk takes in the majority of the city's sights, which lie on the left (west) bank of the Driska and Lielupe rivers. The town has been spruced up in recent years and there are several cafés and restaurants where you can take a break.

Distance: 1.5–2km (1–1¹/₄ miles). Time: allow 2 hours, or 4 hours to delve inside the churches and museums.

1 Statue of Čakstem

This statue of the first ever Latvian President, sculpted by Arta Dumpe, stands proudly in the centre of Jelgava. The fresh flowers by the statue reveal how much he is still revered in Jelgava.
Trīsvienības Laukums.
Cross to the east side of the square.

2 Svētā Trīsvienības Tornis (Holy Trinity Tower)

A rectangular tower behind Čakstem is all that remains of the 17th-century Church of the Holy Trinity.
Trīsvienības Laukums.
Walk south from the square along Akadēmijas Iela for 250m (275yds).

3 Akadēmijas Petrina un Vēstures un Mākslas Muzejs (Academy Petrina and the Museum of History and Art)

This old, largely wooden building built in the neoclassical style is one of the most charming in the city, although in need of renovation. The display in the museum is, however, a lacklustre one of historic furniture.
Akadēmijas Iela 10. Tel: 6302 3383.
Admission charge.
Take the first right after the academy onto Raiņa Iela.

4 Svētā Simeona un Svētās Annas Pareizticīgo Katedrāle (St Simeon and St Anna Orthodox Cathedral)

The striking blue onion domes of this Orthodox church are unmistakable as they rise over Jelgava. Take time to admire the attractive interior, but remember that this is a busy church and cameras are not always welcome.
Raiņa 5. Tel: 6302 0207. Free admission.
Continue 100m (110yds) along the street to the junction with Katolu Iela.

5 Svētā Jura un Svētās Marijas Katoļu Katedrāle (St George and St Maria's Catholic Cathedral)

St Simeon and St Anna's mass of brightly coloured gold-topped domes provides a stark contrast to the Catholic cathedral located on the same street.

Katolu Iela 11. Tel: 6302 1550.

Free admission.

Continue west on Raina Iela, then turn left onto Pastas Iela. Walk 800m (1/2 mile) and turn left onto Stacijas Iela.

6 Latvijas Dzelzceļa Muzeja Filiāle (Railway Museum)

This offbeat little museum by the city's railway station is a must for rail buffs.

Stacijas Iela 3. Tel: 6309 6494.

Admission charge.

Follow Stacijas Iela to the junction with Zemgale Prospekt.

7 Monument to the Liberators of Jelgava

This striking statue, unveiled in 1932, features a stone warrior kneeling with his head bowed. The power in his rippling biceps is meant to convey the strength of the Soviet forces that freed the city from German occupation.

Walk north along Zemgale Prospekt and Akademijas Iela and continue north to the Jelgava Hotel coffee shop on Liela Iela.

Walk: Jelgava tour

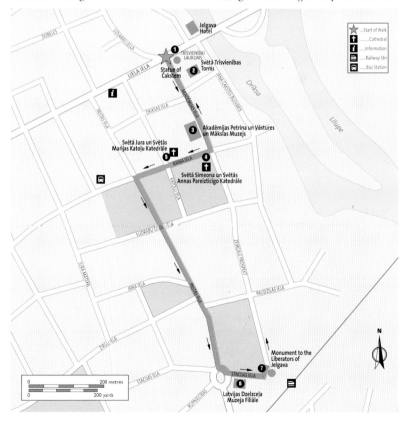

Bauska

The historic town of Bauska has always had a strategic location on key trade routes, as evidenced by the huge castle complex that dwarfs the town. It was originally built by the Livonian Order, but it was the mainstay of Bauska's various rulers over the centuries.
Bauksa Tourist Information Centre, Rātslaukums 1. Tel: 6392 3797. www.tourism.bauska.lv

Bauskas Pils (Bauska Castle)

Bauska's castle has come a long way since it was first erected by the Livonian Order back in the 15th century, and razed to the ground by Peter the Great at the start of the 18th century. Today an ongoing restoration effort is being made to bring the town's landmark

A figure in historical costume at Bauska Castle

back to its best. Its setting is impressive, dominating a massive bluff as you enter Bauska from the south. From the car park a path leads through the woods across the castle's moat and circles the chunky walls. Inside, some of the renovated rooms house a modest museum with figures draped in historical costumes and other displays exploring the castle's history. You can go up one of the fortified towers for sweeping views of the complex, the Mēmele and Mūsa rivers and the surrounding countryside, though the climb up the stairs on the exterior of the tower is not recommended for those who suffer from vertigo.

Bauska Town

If you have the time to spare, the unassuming town of Bauska is worth popping into. A good first stop is the **Bauskas Novadpētniecības un Mākslas Muzejs** (Bauska Museum of Regional Studies). Here you can learn about the history of Bauska as well as the surrounding area from the 18th to the 20th century through the series of old photos that is on display. The rock mound on Kalēju Iela is the subject of a local legend: Peter the Great is said to have dined with the King of Poland at this spot, and the cutlery they used is said to lie beneath. The Church of the Holy Spirit on Pludoņā, built in baroque style with impressive woodwork in the interior, dates back to the 16th century. Just outside Bauska there is a museum dedicated to the local

Bauska Castle is gradually being restored

luminary and celebrated Latvian writer Vilis Pludonis. The museum is housed in the poet's old home and his grave (he died in 1940) is a short stroll away. *Bauska Museum of Regional Studies: Kalna Iela 6. Tel: 6396 0508. www.bauskamuzejs.lv. Admission charge.*

Tērvetes Dabas Parkas
(Tērvete Nature Park)
Easily accessible from Bauska or Jelgava is this very popular nature park. It is not the most spectacular or even one of the largest protected parks in the country, but there are several nature trails that make for a pleasant summer-afternoon stroll. Ornithologists will want to attempt the 'Swan Lake',

which is popular with migrating birds. The 'Fairy Tale' and 'Dwarf' are good for those travelling with children in tow.

LATVIAN BRIGHT SPARKS

Although Latvia is not quite up there with Scotland when it comes to small countries with a penchant for churning out inventors, it boasts a fair few. Apart from Walter Zapp, who invented the tiny Minox camera favoured by James Bond, Latvia is also the birthplace of Jacob W Davis. He was the man who had the ingenuity to hammer rivets onto trousers to make them more durable when he was working with a certain Mr Strauss. Strauss in turn applied for a patent with his business partner, Mr Levi, and the rest made denim history.

Rundāles Pils (Rundāle Palace)

Rundāle is quite simply one of the most striking and impressive palaces in Europe. Its interiors may bear the scars of its turbulent past but the renovated rooms and the grand exterior still stand as a proud testament to rococo and baroque.

Rundāle Palace was commissioned by the Duke of Courland, Ernst Johann von Biron, who envisaged it as his lavish summer getaway. He shipped in the Italian architect Francesco Bartolomeo Rastrelli, who had already proved himself by building the Winter Palace farther east in St Petersburg. Rastrelli began work in 1736, and took five years to complete the palace. He was assisted for the interior by the Italian masters from St Petersburg, Francesco Martini and Carlo Zucchi, and by Johann Michael Graff, the German talent behind the intricate stucco work that gives the palace its sense of drama.

The palace passed through the hands of various baronial owners, each of whom added minor touches of their own and brought in their own period furniture. The onset of World War I saw its darkest hour. Rundāle was damaged during the fighting and fell into disrepair; the post-war years saw it being used as flats and an elementary school.

Rundāle Palace, exterior

The palace's ornate interior

Rundāle was handed over to the state in 1933 as the clouds of war once again circled over Europe, and although it was not badly hit in this second bout of fighting, parts of it were used as a granary for some years after World War II.

It was not until 1972 that Rundāle officially became a museum and serious attempts at restoration began. In total, over 40 rooms have now been painstakingly refurbished out of the original 138, with an attempt to ensure that all of the furnishings and fittings are either 18th-century originals or close to them. These rooms were opened to the public in 1981; the first of the Duke's private apartments was re-opened in 1988, with the Duke's bedroom following in 1990; the first room in the western block, the Duchess' boudoir, was opened for public viewing in 1998. By 2004 the Shuvalov's room and the Duchess' bedroom and toilet room had also been revamped. The meticulous restoration is set to continue as funds come in from the state and from tourist receipts. The palace hosts a number of temporary exhibitions.

Much of the palace grounds have also been brought back to their best along classical French lines, making them a lovely venue for a stroll back through time on a sunny day. Many of the trimmed hedgerows and lime trees are back, and work is still going on. Regular tours to Rundāle run from Rīga, though independent travellers may want to time their visits for early morning or late afternoon to avoid the rush of the tour-bus crowds.

12km (7 miles) west of Bauska.
Tel: 6396 2197. www.rundale.net.
Open: May, Sept–Oct daily 10am–6pm,
June–Aug 10am–7pm, Nov–Apr
10am–5pm. Admission charge.

Mežotnes Pils (Mežotne Palace)

Zemgale's other famous palace lies just a short drive west from Bauska near the banks of the Lielupe River. To some extent it has become a victim of its own success as Mežotne has been transformed from a run-down relic into a glossy hotel and conference facility with manicured English

Mežotne Palace

garden-style grounds, which means that casual visitors are often turned away and not allowed in even for a coffee in the café. Still, if you call ahead this charming palace is well worth visiting, especially if you can combine it with a trip to the more tourist-friendly Rundāle and Bauska.

At first sight Mežotne is not as impressive as Rundāle. This far calmer pastel yellow-hued palace is without the overblown grandeur of its more illustrious neighbour, though no less charming. The palace has a Baltic German heritage, commissioned by Princess Charlotte von Lieven (said to be an ancestor of leading contemporary Baltic expert Anatol Lieven) at the end of the 18th century, after she had been given the land by Catherine the Great.

She was granted the land as a thank you for lending a hand in the education of Catherine's children. Mežotne was completed with impressive speed between 1797 and 1802; in 1799 the Princess von Lieven was awarded the title of Countess.

This Neoclassical gem of a palace suffered, like Rundāle, during the wars and political traumas of the 20th century and it was taken away from the Lievens and used as a post office and apartments. From 1921 to 1943 it even served as an agricultural college. During World War II Mežotne was hit by Red Army artillery fire,

which caused major damage, and by independence in 1991 it was a pale shadow of its former self. After a lot of money and effort went into renovating the palace, work that started in 2001, it is now one of the grandest places to stay in the country, and a venue for large conferences and events. A number of rooms have been revamped, including the lavish ballroom and the much celebrated Cupola Room, with its impressive dome. A popular event held here that is open to all is the annual Festival of Ancient Music (*see p21*), the third week of July. This collage of song, dance and music drawing upon traditional styles from the Renaissance and baroque periods is staged in the atmospheric setting of the palace and its 14 hectares (34 acres) of grounds. The festival also features events at Rundāle Palace and Bauska Castle.

Another way of enjoying the palace is by staying here and following the decadent footsteps of the Baltic German nobility. There are 27 rooms (made up of family rooms, doubles and singles), many with period furnishing, a sauna, a billiards room, restaurant, bar, banquet hall and seven conference rooms, with capacity for 100 delegates.
Tel: 6396 0711.
www.mezotnespils.lv

Fishing on the River Daugava

Up the Daugava

The Daugava is not simply a river but a deeply symbolic site for Latvians, surrounded by myth, intrigue and more than a touch of controversy. Latvia's national epic poem by Andrējs Pumpurs, 'Lāčplēsis' (*The Bear Slayer*), reaches its tragic and heroic denouement on the Daugava, and it was the Daugava that sparked off the first widespread anti-Soviet environmental protests when a hydroelectric project was announced. The protests hit the mark and Moscow relented; now the Daugava is back under Latvian control and the locals revere this mighty waterway more than ever.

Koknese

Follow the main street of Koknese off the main highway from Rīga and you come to the castle where Lāčplēsis was said to have taken on the Black Knight in an epic battle before both died in the Daugava river nearby. The castle ruins are best viewed from the trails that weave around the park. and the photographer's favourite is a shot of the sturdy fortifications mirrored in the water on a sunny day. Pumpurs had Lāčplēsis meeting his fate on the opposite bank of the Daugava, at the impressive Staburags cliff, from where he hurled both himself and the Black Knight to their deaths.

Lielvārde

The old Zemgallian tribal fort as you approach Lielevārde from Rīga may look like an overgrown children's playground, but this was the type of wooden fortress favoured for centuries by the local people until German invaders laid to waste these supposedly impregnable defences by the Daugava. Getting up close to the sharp spikes gives you some idea of the horrors involved in warfare in those days. If there is a school group marauding around the fort, enjoy a coffee in the adjacent café before exploring the fortifications.

On the other side of town, again just off the main highway, is another sturdier-looking fortification. The castle ruins are surrounded by a riverside park in which it's a joy to stroll, taking in the views of the tree-fringed Daugava and checking out the beautifully carved wooden sculptures.

The other attraction here is the **Andrējs Pumpurs Museum**, dedicated to the locally born writer. Pumpurs was the author of the *Lāčplēsis* legend that harks back to Latvian oral legends and celebrates the Latvian national identity. The museum features excerpts and various editions of his work and a range of photographs. Look out for the hulking rock that lies between the museum and the river, which, according to local legend, is where Pumpurs wrote *Lāčplēsis*. A good day to be here is 22 September, Pumpur's birthday, when there are performances and festivities in the park.

Andrējs Pumpurs Museum: Kraujas. Tel: 505 3759. Admission charge.

The Zemgale region

The rugged ruins of Koknese castle

Latgale

Visiting Latgale, with a rural way of life extinct in much of modern Europe, you may be forgiven for thinking that you have stepped back in time. Bicycles are still the main means of transport here and animals continue to play a vital role in farming the land. Driving along Latgale's empty roads, women walking their cows, milk churns being transported by bike or horses drawing ploughs are not an uncommon sight.

Latvia's poorest and least visited region has a mainly Russian population, which is evident in the Soviet architecture and the spoken language (some Latgallians, however, speak in a Latvian dialect that is to many a separate language).

Paradoxically, equally forceful statements of Latvian identity, most visible in the town of Rēzekne (*see pp94–5*) and Catholicism, with ostentatious churches dominating the skylines of many small towns, are also on display.

For most visitors, though, it is the dramatic rural scenery of rolling hills, dense forests and innumerable lakes that is the main attraction of this region.

Jēkabpils

Over the years this attractive town has extended its influence and now occupies both banks of the Daugava river, subsuming neighbouring Krustpils. The majority of Jēkabpils' sights are located south of the river in its baroque old core.

Jēkabpils Tourist Information Centre, Brīvības Iela 140/142. Tel: 6523 382.

Churches

Jēkabpils' compact centre is awash with the spires and onion domes of six churches, places of worship for Orthodox Christians, Lutherans and Baptists. While they are all worth taking a look at, be sure not to miss the two Orthodox churches: the Svētā Gara Pareizticīgo (The Church of the Holy Ghost and monastery) and the Vectincībnieku Baznīca (Old Believer's Church).

Historic houses

The open-air ethnographic and history museum Sēlu Sēta (Selian Farmstead) gives an insight into rural life in the 19th century. On Pastas Iela there are examples of architecture from days gone by: check out the 19th-century houses at No 77/79 and 81/87. On Brīvības Iela, opposite Svētā Nikolaja Brīnumdarītaja Baznīca (the Church of

St Nicholas the Miracle Worker), you will find the town's oldest house that has graced the spot for several centuries.

Krustpils

Looking over Jēkabpils' baroque centre from across the Daugava, you will see Krustpils, which has a handful of attractions of its own – Krustpils Pils (Krustpils Castle), Krustpils Luterāņu Baznīca (Krustpils Lutheran Church), Pemienkils Represiju Upuriem

(Monument to the Victims of Reprisals) and Brīvības Piemineklis (Freedom Monument).

Outdoor spaces

Located just north of Lake Radžu Ūdenskrātuve and dissected by the Daugava River, Jēkabpils is a good place for swimming and boating. Its attractive parks are great places for walking. South of the centre is Jēkabpils Meža Parks (Jēkabpils Forest Park).

Latgale

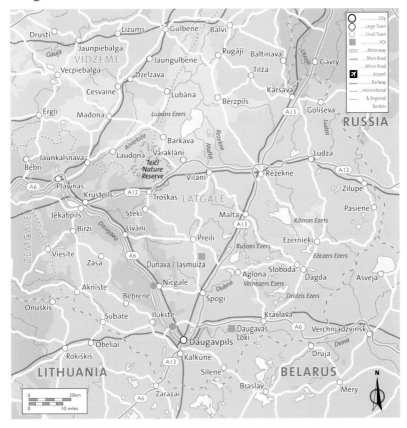

Aglona

Aglona, to many Latvian Catholics, is quite simply the most important place in the country. They flock to the church here in their thousands for epic Masses on key religious dates, especially the Feast of the Assumption on 15 August, when up to 150,000 worshippers descend on this remote corner of Latgale. On the night of 14 August there is an atmospheric torchlit procession. It is not only Latvians who revere Aglona; pilgrims also flood in from neighbouring Lithuania, Belarus and Russia. The village of Aglona itself is pretty unassuming, making the massive cathedral with deep spiritual significance even more dramatic.

Somewhat ironically, the church building stands on the site of what some scholars believe was a pre-Christian sacrificial site. Dominican monks settled in Aglona as far back as the 17th century, but it was not until a century later that the current basilica was erected after fire destroyed its wooden predecessor in 1766. Today's Baroque-style basilica was built between 1768 and 1780 and was consecrated in 1800, and is dedicated to the Assumption of the Virgin Mary.

The setting is very picturesque, with the church and monastery buildings resting amidst thick forest backed by lakes (the Aglona itself and the Cirīšs). Indeed, the name

Aglona's starched white church

Aglona is said to derive from the Latvian for 'pine forest'.

The church building is a striking white hue, with two sinuous towers over 50m (164ft) tall. It is surrounded by a large park where the faithful flock on key dates and manage to fill up the vast grounds; for the rest of the year the church is closed to visitors. There is no real schedule for opening outside religious ceremonies.

Much of Aglona's spiritual importance comes from the image of the Virgin Mary installed in the interior, which is said to possess miraculous powers; it is even believed to have saved the town from the plague at one point. However, even when the church is open the image, placed in one of the ten altars, may not be on display. The painting is believed to date to the 17th century and it bears an inscription which reads 'This is the true painting of the Aglona Mother of God which for 134 years has been famous for miracles.' The church's reputation was further enhanced in 1798 when a Latvian woman claimed to have seen an image of the Virgin nearby.

During Soviet times, when religion was very much frowned upon if not suppressed, Aglona was closed down with its priests and nuns expelled, public transport to the site banned and the historic Dominican library destroyed. The basilica itself fell into a state of disrepair. After Latvian independence, though, the church was extensively refurbished and its renaissance was crowned by a triumphant visit from Pope John Paul II in 1993, the man who gave it the status of a basilica in 1980, on its bicentenary. In 1986, the 800th anniversary of Christianity in Latvia was also celebrated at Aglona.

Sculpted detail from the church

Rēzekne

People who arrive in Rēzekne expecting to see scenes of communist deprivation and monotonous high-rise concrete blocks are often pleasantly surprised by this attractive and fairly prosperous town, laid out on a neat grid.

Latgales Kultūrvēstures Muzejs (Latgale Museum of Cultural History)

In this museum dedicated to the history of pottery-making and of Rēzekne, you will find attractive ceramics alongside photographs of the local woman who posed for the Māra sculpture and images of the city before World War I.

Atbrivoshanas Aleja 102.
Tel: 462 2464.

Latgales Māra (Māra of Latgale)

Situated on the main Atbrīvošanas Aleja square, also a busy traffic roundabout, the statue of Latgales Māra watches protectively over the town. Erected in 1939 in celebration of emancipation from the rule of the Bolsheviks in January 1920, the statue has come to symbolise freedom from foreign powers. It also rapidly evolved into a symbol of Latvian independence, a sentiment that outraged the occupying Russians who demanded its removal in 1940. When Europe was in the throes of war the statue was resurrected in 1943, only to be removed once again by the Russians in 1950.

Shortly after the dawn of Latvian independence, Latvia's earth mother was resurrected for a final time in August 1992.

The Latgales Māra is an imposing statue of a powerful matriarch who, standing atop a large concrete pillar inscribed *Vienoti Latvijai* (For United Latvia), raises a cross defiantly towards the sky, while a male warrior lies at her feet. The strong feminine symbolism is reminiscent of the Freedom Monument in Rīga.

The choice of Māra, a Latvian goddess traditionally associated with peace and nature, was to some Latvians a strange one.

Monument to the Liberators of Rēzekne

One of Latvia's few surviving Soviet memorials stands in the centre of town. Sculpted by Kaleys, Silinysh and Salguss, the statue was unveiled in 1976 and is a tribute to the Soviet soldiers who freed the city from Nazi occupation in 1944.

Junction of Latgales Iela and Atbrivoshanas Aleja.

Places of worship

Like most Latvian towns, Rēzekne has a collection of churches, the most impressive among them being the small but immaculate Orthodox church and the city's Catholic church, both occupying the same square (Atbrīvošanas Aleja).

The former has the signature Orthodox white walls and blue onion domes, while flowers adorn the door

A verdant setting for Rēzekne Orthodox Church

and lead into the church. Rēzekne's Catholic church is an attractive white building with two steeples and a small statue of Christ on the roof. On the outskirts of the town there is also an enormous red-brick Catholic cathedral.

Ruined fortress

Little remains of Rēzekne's once powerful Latgallian medieval castle.

Later a stronghold of the German Knights, the fortress was abandoned in the 17th century, with the stones gradually being removed to construct buildings elsewhere in the town. The castle hill is still worth visiting, though, not only to see the ruins that have survived, but also for the elevated view that takes in the Catholic cathedral.

Ludza's Catholic church

Ludza

Arguably the prettiest settlement in Latgale and one of Latvia's oldest towns, this is an essential stopover. Ludza is framed by three lakes – Lielais Ludzas Ezers (Big Ludza Lake), Mazais Ludzas Ezers (Little Ludza Lake) and Dunaklu Ezers (Lake Dunaklu) – and thick forest. Only a half-hour drive east of Rēzekne towards the Russian border, it enjoys an attractive setting that is backed by a phalanx of pretty wooden houses, an easily navigable old core, a couple of interesting churches and an impressive ruined castle. This was once a key stronghold of the powerful

Latgale tribe, whose distinctive culture and traditions live on in the hearts and minds of many locals even today, though the Germans and Poles swept through the town over the years. Ludza remained under Polish control until the division of Poland in 1771 ceded it to Russia.
Ludza Tourist Information Centre, Baznīca Iela 42. Tel: 6570 720. www.ludza.lv

Ludza castle

This old red-brick fortress is one of the most dramatic in Latvia, with atmospheric ruins standing proudly on a grassy knoll. Originally a wooden fortress, built by the indigenous Latgallian tribes, the strategic site was seized by marauding German Knights who at the end of the 14th century built the castle whose remains you see today. From the old keep you can walk around the outer walls of the castle to take in views of the town and surrounding lakes.

Ludza churches

With its white sheen and vaulting twin towers, Ludza's Catholic church at Baznīcas Iela 54, just across from the castle, is reminiscent of the famous church at Aglona, though on a much smaller scale. It was renovated in the mid-1990s and the interior is notable for its impressive wooden sculptures. The Orthodox Church in the town centre at Latgales Iela 121 has Russian classical pale-yellow lower sections which contrast in hue markedly from its bright-blue onion domes. This charming building was completed in 1845 and is now a protected national monument.

The dramatic ruins of Ludza castle

An unspoilt Latgale lake, a haven for wildlife

Ludzas Novadpētniecības Muzejs (Ludza District Museum)

The district museum is housed in a 14th-century wooden house in the centre of town, which used to belong to an 18th-century war hero. Here you can explore Ludza's eclectic history through a sprinkling of artefacts ranging from military memorabilia through to jewellery. The museum contains the fruits of archaeological digs in the surrounding area which shed light on the early Latgallian tribes, as well as an old house, barn and windmill. Behind the museum is a small Jewish graveyard, a testament to the once thriving local Jewish community that was swept away by Nazism in 1941. *Kuļņeva Iela 2. Tel: 572 3931. Admission charge.*

Activities in Ludza district

Ludza district is one of the most unspoilt areas in the country. There are around 140 lakes of all shapes and sizes, and around a third of the territory is swathed in pine and fir forests. Walking and cycling tours are both popular here; ask at the tourist office in Ludza for seasonal details. There is also a small beach at Lielais Ludzas in Ludza with some facilities in summer.

The Latgale lakes

Latgale, the 'Land of Blue Lakes', as its name suggests is a region overflowing with lakes (the majority of the country's 2,000-plus lakes are located here). They come in all shapes and sizes: from little pools no bigger than a pond to Lake Lubāns, the largest of them all. This area sees few international guests, but a large number of Latvians are in on the secret and head out to waterside campsites, B&Bs and holiday log cabins, especially in the summer. Many of the roads leading here are still dirt tracks; this keeps trucks and tour buses away, leaving you to explore on your own, unfettered by crowds. One thing to bear in mind is that many of the prettiest lakes are hidden by trees; so, if you catch a glimpse of an attractive stretch of water from your car window you should stop and investigate.

There are plenty of opportunities for rowing, fishing (for pike, eel and zander), cycling and mountain biking. Things tend to be very much on a smaller local scale compared to the big tour operators, so check out the facilities and activities available at the local tourist offices in Daugavpils and Rēzekne.

Ežezers Ezers (Lake Ežezers)

The 'Hedgehog Lake' is another fine place to relax, surrounded by clean waters and pine trees. Locals boast that this is the most attractive lake in the country, and many visitors find it hard to disagree. The lake sports no fewer than 36 islands (more than any other lake in Latvia) and you can take a boat out to explore them for yourself.

Lubāns Ezers (Lake Lubāns)

Lubāns used to be Latvia's largest lake until it was partially drained as part of an unpopular Soviet-era industrial project. It was almost twice the size of Rāzna, at over 90sq km (35sq miles), until the Soviets siphoned off much of its body. Today it has recovered to around 80sq km (31sq miles), which makes it again the country's largest lake. It is popular with migratory birds and hence with ornithologists who come here every spring and autumn.

Rāznas Ezers (Lake Rāzna)

Rāzna, at over 50sq km (19sq miles) enjoyed a spell as Latvia's largest lake (*see above*) and it is still popular with visitors, especially in summer, who come to canoe, fish and swim in its waters. Due to its size there is always somewhere to escape the crowds and enjoy this still unspoilt lake and the surrounding rolling countryside. Its eastern and southern shores are the most popular and easiest to get to.

Other lakes

There are many more lakes in Latgale to choose from, including: Dridzis, which, at 63m (207ft) in depth, is not only the deepest lake in Latvia but anywhere in the Baltics; Velnezers, which translates literally as 'Devil Lake', a name earned by its unusual hues and the multitude of legends that surround its mysterious banks; and Lake Rušons, which is another lake renowned for its beauty.

Russian Latvians

The status of the Russian-speaking population within Latvia is one of the most controversial and inflammatory issues in Latvian society and politics today. There had always been cross-border movement between the two countries, but this rapidly escalated after World War II, when the Soviet Union decided to use Latvian territory for establishing heavy industry and brought in Soviet workers, dramatically changing Latvia's demographic profile.

The years after the war saw a further inflow of industrial plants and projects and, with them, a large supply of cheap labour from the Russian heartland. By the 1980s ethnic Latvians had effectively become a minority in their own country and

Russian Orthodox Cathedral, Rīga

there was a clearly discernible policy of 'Russification' with Moscow hoping it could integrate the entire population into Mother Russia. Many of the Russian immigrants often made little attempt to learn the local language or customs; they were backed by the Moscow-guided authorities who gave them little encouragement to integrate. Matters came to a head in 1991 when this Russian-speaking population (numbering almost one million out of a total Latvian population of only 2.4 million) were caught between loyalty to the dissolving Soviet Union and the newly independent Latvia.

Some of the Russian speakers chose to leave, but those who stayed soon discovered that their status as citizens of the new Latvia was by no means guaranteed. Latvians were not prepared to forgive and forget the decades of Soviet suppression and discrimination in economic and political life, and, to some extent, there was a real fear of this volatile Russian community who still held significant power within the country. The result was a new law that defined who could and who could not be a Latvian citizen – a similar law was passed in Estonia but not in Lithuania.

An exhibition exploring Soviet history and the occupation of Latvia

This post-independence legislation stated that Russian-speakers who had been born or were descendants of anyone who had been born in Latvia prior to World War II qualified automatically for full Latvian citizenship. Those who did not automatically qualify had to go through new Latvian language and Latvian history exams, as well as learn the country's national anthem. If they failed these exams or refused to take them, they were still allowed to live in Latvia, but effectively as 'stateless' residents. They were, and are, allowed many of the rights given to other Latvian citizens, but not eligibility to vote in elections or referendums.

This policy drew widespread criticism from much of Europe and the USA, and Latvia has since softened some of the restrictions on its non-citizens. For example, since 2002 they have been allowed to hold political office. Now that Latvia has become a member of the European Union, these non-citizen Russian speakers, making up around 30 per cent of the population, are effectively third-country citizens living in the European Union, as they are neither Latvian nor European. Unlike the Latvians they live and work with, they cannot work elsewhere in the EU though they do enjoy visa-free travel into Russia. The issue thus remains a thorny one, especially in a country where 9 May is seen by some as a great celebration of victory over Nazism and by others as the start of the tragic Soviet occupation. In 2006, the Russian president stoked the situation by initiating a programme designed to attract ethnic Russians back to the mother country.

Drive: Around Latgale

Latgale is a region of rough roads and maniac drivers, but for the brave the gently rolling countryside is perfect for exploring by car; just make sure you are armed with full car insurance. This driving route travels south from Līvāni to Daugavpils, Latvia's second largest city, and then east to Krāslava.

Distance: 120km (75 miles). Time: allow 10 hours, if you want time to explore the settlements, museum and nature park on this route.

From Jēkabpils head south on the A6 to Līvāni, 30–40 minutes' drive.

1 Līvāni

If you are interested in glassware, the modest village of Līvāni (*www.livani.lv*) is the place to stop. The skill of the local glassblowers is legendary and you can pick up interesting items in the store that sells their work. Also check out the traditional craft displays at the Līvānu Novada Amatniecības Centrs

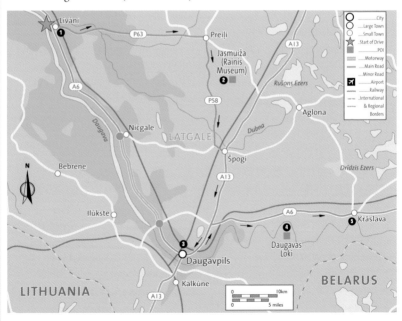

(*Līvāni Domes Iela 1; tel: 538 1855*),
where pottery and weaving
demonstrations take place.
It is advisable to call ahead.
*Head 30km (19 miles) east to Preiļi on
the P63 then due south for 8km (5 miles)
to Jasmuiža on the P58.*

2 Jasmuiža (Rainis Museum)

This picturesque park and rural cottage
on the banks of the Jasna River is an
essential stop for anyone interested in
the life and work of the beloved Latvian
playwright and poet Jānis Rainis, who
championed the national cause and use
of the Latvian language (*see p49 &
p121*). A large exhibition of ceramics is
open to visitors, and on Sunday
afternoons you can often see potters
demonstrating their skills.
*Aizkalnes pagasts. Tel: 6532 9313.
Admission charge.*
*Return to the P58 and continue south
until you join the A13 to Daugavpils.
Allow 30 minutes.*

3 Daugavpils

Of interest only to those with a
penchant for heavy industry and
Soviet-era architecture, Latvia's brash
second city is ignored by most visitors.
It is worth a brief stop, though, to
witness this Russian-dominated city
struggling to follow Rīga, Ventspils
and Liepāja in forging a new role for
itself in post-independence Latvia.
For more information about the
city, visit the Tourist Information
Centre (*Rīgas Iela 22a; tel: 542 2818*).

*Leaving the maelstrom of Daugavpils,
follow the A6 to Daugavas Loki.*

4 Daugavas Loki

This nature and cultural park
showcases one of the most spectacular
stretches of the Daugava River, which
makes nine sweeping bends within
the reserve. Daugavas Loki is popular
with Latgallian families who take to
its waters on warm summer weekends.
To really appreciate the park, hire a
dugout canoe from one of the various
rental locations, or spend a night at
one of its camping grounds. An
open-air museum and castle mound
are amongst the park's cultural
attractions.
*Return to the A6 and continue in
an easterly direction to Krāslava.
Travelling directly from Daugavpils to
Krāslava takes about an hour.*

5 Krāslava

This unassuming town lies right on
Latvia's border with Lithuania and is
only a stone's throw from the Russian
border too. It was once a major trading
centre, thanks to its strategic position,
but it has since fallen into decline. Its
most charming features are an 18th-
century castle, which houses a museum
dedicated to local arts and history, and
traditional wooden houses. Look out
for the 18th-century Catholic church
on Puškina, commissioned as the seat
of the Bishop of Latgale.
*Krāslava Muzejs: Pils Iela 8.
Tel: 562 3586. Admission charge.*

Vidzeme

Situated to the northeast of Rīga, this easily accessible region has a dramatic Baltic Sea coast with pristine white sands flanked by tall pines. In the height of the tourist season and on sunny weekends the coast comes alive as city dwellers leave the capital in droves. In the north, towards the Estonian border, the coast is wilder with windswept beaches. Vidzeme, like Latgale, is also a region of hills and dense forests, with nature trails perfect for a quiet escape.

One truly unique feature of Vidzeme is that it houses Latvia's only Biosphere Reserve (*see p143*). This large reserve (which covers approximately five per cent of the country's territory) protects woodland, coastal and marine habitats. Another of Vidzeme's attractions is its vast waterways; the Gauja River and its tributaries (*see pp112–19*) are just some of the places where you can take to the water or indulge in some fishing. Its lakes, rivers and forests make Vidzeme an ideal rural retreat where you can rent a remote log cabin and escape the modern world.

It is not only Vidzeme's natural bounty that gives it a special place in the heart of Latvians, but also its historical towns, ancient castles and rich cultural traditions. During local fiestas it is not unusual to see people wearing traditional garments. A historic fisherman's festival is held every July in settlements along the coast.

The most visited of Vidzeme's urban centres are Sigulda (*pp110–11*) and

Cēsis (*see below*); the town of Limbaži (*see pp122–3*), which has a history that dates back to the beginning of the 13th century, and the lake fortress at Āraiši (*see p114*) are other highlights. It is almost as if every settlement in Vidzeme had its own castle or castle mound, the most impressive structures being Turaida Castle (*see p115*) and the imposing fortress ruins at Cēsis (*see p106*).

Cēsis

History

As one of Latvia's oldest towns, Cēsis commands a central place in Latvian history and in national consciousness. In 2006 the town celebrated its 800th anniversary and its role in shaping Latvia, including its membership of the Hanseatic League, in the creation of the Latvian flag and in the establishment of the country's oldest brewery.

The medieval castle, which stood as a bulwark for 500 years, was subjected to attacks by Russian, Polish and Swedish forces as well as German troops during the Livonian War in the 13th century. Abandoned at the outset of the Great Nordic War (1703), the castle fell into ruin, regaining its place at the centre of Cēsis' cultural life almost 300 years later. The town's other ancient monuments also testify to Cēsis' rich history, while its attractive parks and clean streets are its citizens' civic pride.

Cēsis is a particularly rewarding place to visit when its streets and the open-air auditorium in Pils Park come alive with one of many cultural events. Look out for flyers advertising performances by the esteemed Latvian State Opera.

Cīsu Jaunā Pils (Cēsis New Castle)

Even if you don't visit the museum inside (*see p109*), the castle is still worth a visit for its architecture. This ornate manor house was constructed on the site of the old castle's gates in the late 18th century. The new castle has a relatively short but chequered history; it has been used as a family home, sanatorium and even an officers' mess during Soviet times.

Pils Laukums 9. Tel: 6412 2615.

Cēsu Izstāžu nams (Exhibition Hall)

Housed in the former stables of Cēsis New Castle, the Exhibition Hall is a

Vidzeme

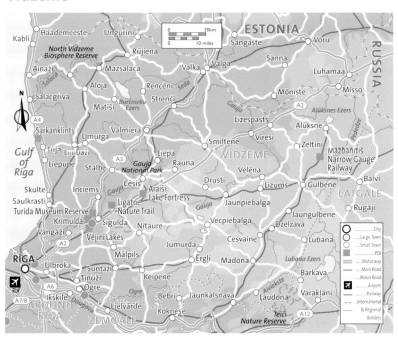

central venue for art exhibitions
and concerts.
Pils Laukums 3. Tel: 6412 3557.

Livonijas Ordeņa Cēsu Mūra Pils
(Cēsis Castle of the Livonian Order)
This 800-year-old fortress is impressive
in both scale and appearance. The
castle's western and southern towers,
both added in the 16th century, remain
largely intact. Visitors can explore the
dungeon housed in the south tower.
Pils Laukums 11. Tel: 6412 2615.

May Park
This pleasant little park was created in
the 19th century, and its most bizarre
feature is a castle ruin, constructed to
keep it in step with the larger Pils Park.
Attractive flower beds, an artificial
pond and Kārlis Janson's sculpture,
Battle with the Centaur, now one of the
town's most well-known emblems, can
also be found here.
Lielā Katrīnas Iela.

Old brewery
Although historical records indicate
that there has been a brewery in Cēsis
since the late 16th century, the existing
old brewery in the town dates from the
19th century. Beer is also brewed at a
new plant on the outskirts of Cēsis.
It is the country's second-largest beer
producer and its oldest.

Rīgas Iela (Rīga Street)
The town's main artery for over 700
years, Rīgas Iela is home to some of
Cēsis' oldest buildings: the Rathaus at
No 7, the Trader's House at No 16,
the Harmony House at No 24 and the
Princesses' Manor at No 47. At the end
of the street you can also see Rauna
Gate, the only surviving portal of the
town's medieval walls.

Ūndens Iela (Water Street)
Running north to south between
Vaļņu Iela and Rīgas Iela is a small
street with diverse examples of
architecture. Look out for the part-
wood/part-stone house whose upper
floor overhangs the ground floor.
Ūndens is also notable as one of the
few central streets that is still paved
with traditional cobbles.

Cēsis Castle, Vidzeme

Cēsis Castle of the Livonian Order, one of Latvia's most impressive

Vienības Laukums (Union Square)

Cēsis' newest and largest square is notable not only for the Victory Monument (*see p108*) but also the impressive 19th-century courthouse.

Surrounding area

Due to its location at the heart of the Gauja National Park, various outdoor activities can be enjoyed near Cēsis (*see pp116–17*). There are opportunities for visiting farms, museums, churches, castles and the subterranean lakes at Vējiņi (the only ones of their kind in Latvia). For more information, contact the Cēsis Tourist Information Centre (*Pils Laukums 1; tel: 6412 1815; www.tourism.cesis.lv*).

Walk: Cēsis

If you only have time to visit one place outside of Rīga then Cēsis is a keen contender. This walk around historic Cēsis skirts the main sights and offers the chance to discover a lot more than just the landmark castle that is the town's main attraction.

Distance: 2.5–3km (1½–2 miles). Time: allow at least 2 hours.

The route can be covered in an afternoon at a push, but it is best to take your time and soak in the atmosphere. Note that the descent to the gardens below the castle is quite steep and the way back up is a hike too.

The grand Vienības Laukums (Union Square) is the best place to begin.

1 Uzvaras Piemineklis (Victory Monument)

This grand, if not charming, memorial to the Battle of Cēsis dominates the

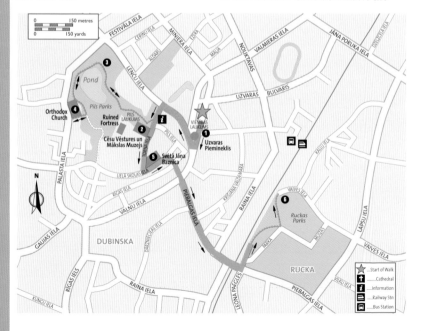

town's central square. Although much revered by the citizens of Cēsis, the Soviets did not take kindly to its pro-Latvian theme and demolished it in 1951. It reappeared in its present incarnation in 1998.

Vienības Laukums.

From the square head northwest along Lenču Iela and then take the second left past the tourist information centre. Walk southwest until you reach Pils Laukums.

2 Cēsu Vēstures un Mākslas Muzejs (Cēsis Museum of History and Art)

Housed in the 'new castle' adjunct to Cēsis' ruined fortress, this museum reveals the eclectic history of this ancient town. Exhibits date back as far as the 11th century BC. The highlight for many is climbing to the top of Lademahers Tower, from where expansive views of the town unfurl.

Pils Laukums 9. Tel: 6412 2615. Admission charge.

Head west across the courtyard and follow the steps down to the castle gardens.

3 Pils Parks (Castle Gardens)

Below the castle ramparts are well laid out gardens. Walking trails lead off from the park, but beware taking the one that looks like a shortcut back to the castle as it is a dead end. As you descend the stairs to the park, look out for the sculptures of children.

Walk anticlockwise around the pond, then head south to the Orthodox Church.

4 Orthodox Church

This relic of Russian rule has classic onion domes.

Retrace your steps back towards the pond and head east to the steps which take you past the new castle and onto Torņa Iela. Follow Torņa Iela in a southwesterly direction until you reach the junction with Lielā Skolas Iela. Turn left.

5 Svētā Jāņa Baznīca (St John's Church)

This huge church in the town centre has dominated one of the most charming parts of Cēsis since the late 13th century. It is well worth visiting as it houses many tombs of the knights and rulers of the Livonian Order – reminders of the town's former wealth and importance. The most famous of the nobles interred here is Walter von Plettenburg, who battled against the Russian threat in the 16th century.

Lielā Skolas Iela 8. Tel: 6412 4448.

Head northeast along Lielā Skolas Iela. Take the first right and follow Piebalgas Iela south to Parka. Turn left for Ruckas Park.

6 Ruckas Parks (Ruckas Park)

If the tourist crowds get too much in summer you can head out to this quieter little park.

To return to Vienības Laukums head north up Piebalgas Iela, turning right at Valnu Iela.

Sigulda

Sigulda is a town with an attractive collection of country houses, green spaces and tree-shrouded streets. The old and new castles at its heart are the real highlights, alongside the dramatic views of the Gauja Valley afforded by this part of town. Although just 50km (31 miles) from Rīga, Sigulda feels a million miles away from the capital's frenetic city streets. Here life passes by at a pleasant pace, making this tranquil retreat an ideal place to base your explorations of the Gauja National Park (*see pp112–19*).
Sigulda Tourist Information Centre, Valdemara Iela 1a. Tel: 6797 1335. www.sigulda.lv

Colourful gardens brighten up the popular tourist town of Sigulda

Artist's Hill

Artist's Hill (93m/305ft above sea level), on the eastern fringes of the town, is not high by world standards, but it does afford views that extend to around 10km (6 miles).

Cable car

From Poruka Iela 14 you can take one of the hourly cable cars to Krimulda Castle. This is well worth it for the treetop panoramic view over the Gauja Valley and the snaking Gauja River.

Knights' Castle

Directly opposite Sigulda's new castle are the unmistakable ruins of the old fort. This amber-coloured structure was a Liv stronghold back in the 13th century. Despite its size and high (for Latvia) location, the castle was overrun and destroyed on several occasions during its history. Last sacked during the Northern Wars that raged in the region between 1700 and 1721, the castle was never rebuilt. Of the remnants, the main keep and watchtowers are still an impressive sight. The trails that lead off from the castle afford glimpses of Turaida Castle (*see p115*) on the other side of the river; many of the views, however, are hidden by the trees that crowd this verdant part of Latvia.

Luterāņu Baznīca (Lutheran Church)

The green park that houses Sigulda's Lutheran church renders its brilliant white walls even more striking. It is

The Knights' Castle in Sigulda has been sympathetically restored

notable for its attractive exterior, typical of the smaller rural churches in the Baltic region. The church has stood on the spot since 1225, but numerous alterations over the years lend it a more modern appearance.
Baznīcas Iela 2.

Monument to Krišjānis Barons

At the intersection of Pils Iela and Līvkalna Iela you will find an impressive sculpture designed by Teodors Zaļkalns. The statue is a tribute to one of the country's best-loved poets and folklorists, Krišjānis Barons.

New Castle

This impressive 19th-century mansion houses the town's best restaurant (*see p165*), whose terrace and window tables offer spectacular views of the ruins of the old castle, and Sigulda's council offices. Take time to walk around the exterior of the castle, stopping to admire the panoramic views of the Gauja Valley and the neat flowerbeds. The statue in front of the manor is of the writer Atis Kronvalds who pushed for the use of Latvian in schools in the mid-19th century.
Pils Iela 16.

Sigulda bobsleigh and sleigh track

For a white-knuckle experience, ride the fast-paced tourist bobsleigh.
Check at the Tourist Information Centre for details. Closed: Apr.

THE GAUJA NATIONAL PARK

Gauja is a lush, green protected national park just an hour's drive from Rīga. Locals like to call it 'Latvia's Switzerland', which, of course, it is not, as this is not a country of Alpine peaks. Instead, it is very Latvian – a clean and green oasis filled with opportunities to get close to Mother Nature, whether it be setting out on the walking trails taking in the fresh air and sights, cruising down the Gauja River on a canoe, or, for adrenaline junkies, flinging yourself out of a cable car with only a bungee rope for company.

Whatever your penchant, it would take the most hardhearted city-slicker not to enjoy a natural haven that sums up so much of what is good about Latvia.

Trail through the Gauja National Park

Gauja National Park was conceived as recently as 1973 (environmental protection not often having been a priority for the Soviet authorities) and it has not looked back since, quickly winning a place in the hearts of most Latvians and increasingly of foreign visitors. Comprising more than 920sq km (355sq miles) of land, most of the park is open to visitors, though a few areas are off limits, and used instead for conservation and scientific research. Visitors can while away the hours here following woodland nature trails and canoeing along the mighty Gauja River – 425km (264 miles) long, it is the longest river in Latvia.

Flora and fauna

Apart from the Gauja, tributary rivers and streams such as the Amata and Brasla also run through the park. Almost half the park territory is forest-covered, with the dense rows of pines and spruces (you can also see lime, ash and oak trees) providing the perfect habitat for numerous mammal species and a diverse range of plants. Beyond the trees that line the river banks, the park has agricultural plains, meadows with attractive spring flowers, small lakes and peat bogs. Together these diverse habitats support around 1,000 types of flora, 149 species of birds, 50 different mammals, small amphibians, moss, lichen and over 400 varieties of fungi.

The most commonly spotted animals include otters and the roe deer, elk, red deer and wild boar. Ornithologists have reported sighting rare birds like lesser-spotted eagles, pygmy owls and black storks; ducks, loons, Canada geese, robins, jays, storks and herons are more commonly seen. The waterways themselves are home to salmon, pike and trout.

Cultural heritage

There is more to the park than the conservation of nature. The indelible imprint of man forms part of the attraction too. Inside the park there are around 500 historical buildings and cultural monuments, including ruined castles, castle mounds, churches, grand manor houses and old windmills. Each monument tells its own story about how passing generations of people lived. The historic towns of Cēsis (*see pp104–9*) and Sigulda (*see pp110–11*) are also protected by the national park.

The Gauja River flows through thick forests rich with wildlife

Āraiši Lake Fortress

Seven kilometres (4 miles) south of Cēsis is the picturesque Āraiši Lake where reconstructed log huts huddle together on a small islet. Collectively these 15 dwellings comprise the Āraiši Lake Fortress. The original homes that stood here back in the 9th and 10th centuries acted as a line of defence. You can step back in time and travel to the fortress in a traditional dugout canoe (*for details tel: 6419 7288*).

Archaeological objects

Preservation of the 20m (66ft) high Zvārtes Rock, which juts out from the

Dramatic sculpture in the Turaida Sculpture Park

banks of the Amata River, was considered so important that the water flow was changed in 1933 to stop it from being partially submerged. Latvian folklore claims that the rock was the secret meeting place for witches at Christmas and on Jānu Diena or 'St John's Day' (*see p21*). The white sandstone Sietiņiezis Rock, believed to be around 300 million years old, and the country's highest sandstone cliff (Ērgļu Klintis) are two of the park's precious sights.

Events

In almost every month of the year the park authorities organise an event in a bid to attract more visitors, and to give repeat visitors the chance to participate in something more unusual. Events so far have included carnival processions at Turaida Castle, Easter celebrations, free access to the Līgatne trails (*see pp118–19*), craft fairs and activities linked to the birds and fish that pass through the park on their migration routes.

Krimulda

Accessed by a steep walking trail or cable car from Sigulda, Krimulda boasts a small collection of old stone houses, a ruined castle (Krimuldas Pilsdrupas), large oak trees and an impressive palace built in classical style (now a children's sanatorium). The real reason to visit Krimulda, however, is for the dramatic hilltop views over the Gauja Valley and for the treetop cable-car ride to Sigulda.

Turaida Museum Reserve

This protected area, 3km (2 miles) north of Sigulda, is one of Latvia's most visited tourist sites. People flock here especially to see the eponymous castle, its most historic and striking attraction. The reconstructed castle commands an enviable position perched on an outcrop overlooking the Gauja River. Originally a wooden Liv fortress, it has undergone many makeovers through the centuries as it attempted to make a comeback from assaults, in particular a catastrophic wound in the 18th century when its armoury took a direct hit from a bolt of lightning.
Turaidas Iela 10. Tel: 6797 1420. www.turaida-muzej.lv

Turaida Castle

The red-brick castle is Turaida Reserve's star, although its reconstruction, which began in the 1950s, may not be to everyone's taste. The views from the lookout point way up one of the trio of towers are superb, opening up whole vistas of the Gauja National Park.

Turaida's other attractions

Don't leave the reserve without exploring its lazy trails. Look out for the small, wooden, 18th-century Turaidas Baznīca (Turaida Church) on the way between the castle and the main gate, and also for the sculptures that dot the pathways, based on Latvian folk stories and legends.

Storks are a common sight in the Latvian countryside

Getting active

Canoeing

The Gauja River provides the best vantage point from which to appreciate the park's natural beauty; it allows you to get close to the sandstone caves, rocks and cliffs that punctuate its banks. A real highlight is the stretch of the river which runs between Cēsis and Sigulda; a leisurely canoe or kayak trip between the two towns takes two to three days. More experienced kayakers can enjoy the thrills of the fast-flowing early spring waters that occur when the melting snow causes the river to swell. Others might prefer to wait until early summer when the Gauja's pace slows to a gentle meander. Those with less time on their hands could consider renting a Canadian canoe for a paddle around Lake Āraiši (*see p114*) or Lake Vaidava.

Hiking

Walkers have two options in the park: to follow the well-trodden way-marked tourist trails; or to book a park guide with the option of camping in the wild on longer routes.

Tourist trails The Gauja National Park has over 100km (62 miles) of established trails, most of which are straightforward to follow and relatively flat, making them suitable for anyone with a reasonable level of fitness. Along the trails, which take in natural sights like the Sietiņiezis Rock and the Ērgļu cliffs (*see p115*), as well as historic monuments and settlements like Turaida Castle (*see p115*) and Cēsis (*see pp104–9*), there are a number of basic campsites where you can pitch a tent without being charged.

Guided walks Under the expert guidance of a park official it is possible to access almost any part of the park. Those who are not too keen on the idea of camping in the wild or following unmarked trails can hire the services of a guide who will be able to give detailed information about the places they visit, the ecology of the park, and the fauna and flora. If you want to go on a guided expedition, it is wise to organise this in advance and to clarify the cost, group size, route requirements and language that you wish to be guided in.

Cycling
Many of the trails for walkers are also accessible to cyclists. Contact the park administration for information about routes and bike hire. One very popular route runs from Cēsis (*see pp134–6*).

Skiing
From late November through to March, trade in your walking boots for cross-country skis to explore the park as it takes on the feel of a winter wonderland.

Staying in the park
There are dozens of campsites located on the banks of the Gauja, Amata and Brasla. Most of these can be reached by canoe; some are also accessible by bicycle, foot or car. Camping is usually free of charge and there is no need to book in advance. You can also pitch your tent anywhere you want to in the park, as long as it is not in a restricted area.

Further information
To learn more about the Gauja National Park, contact the Administration and Visitor Centre (*Baznīcas Iela 3, Sigulda; tel: 797 4006; www.gnp.lv*).

Enjoying a canoe trip on the Gauja River in the National Park

Walk: Līgatne Nature Trail

The Līgatne Nature Trail is a self-guided walking route with a difference. As you follow the path you will come across a number of enclosures that allow you to get close to some of Latvia's indigenous animals.

The trail extends for about 5km (3 miles). Allow 2–3 hours for a leisurely stroll and enough time to see the animals.

Head south from the Visitor Centre across the car park to the beginning of the trail, which involves a gentle ascent amidst dense forest.

1 The forest
Take time to admire the tall pine and spruce trees, and look for birds of prey.

A wolf dog on the Līgatne nature trail

Follow the trail southwest, and you will soon reach the first enclosure, which houses 'wolf dogs'.

2 Wolf dogs
Līgatne's 'wolf dogs' are a hybrid that emerged from the mating of dog and wolf. If you whistle they may come to the fence like obedient dogs in hope of food, but the English and Latvian signs warn that they are a menace in rural communities and are more likely to attack domestic pets than wolves. *Following the trail southwest, you will soon reach the bear enclosure, a circular clearing amidst the trees.*

3 Brown bears
The bears can be viewed from two platforms. This is the most disturbing part of the walk, as the enclosure is small and bereft of trees, while an expansive wood lies tauntingly out of reach. This is a rare chance to see the brown bear which was once extinct in Latvia; it also lives in the wild in Latvia.

4 Taking the short route/owls

From the bear enclosure those short of time can visit the owls and then retrace their steps to the car park. Enclosures are not ideal for owls as they are unable to follow their nocturnal hunting instincts.

5 Red deer

If you want to see all the animals in the park you will need to follow the path from the owls to the red deer via the wild boars.

From the red deer follow the nature trail east.

6 Aurochs

Although aurochs (European bison) roam freely in the Pape National Park (*see pp76–7*), few visitors are lucky enough to see them there.

At the auroch enclosure follow the path winding in a northwesterly direction.

7 Completing the circuit

You will pass the foxes and raccoon dogs before you reach the owls. From here you need to retrace your steps to the car park.

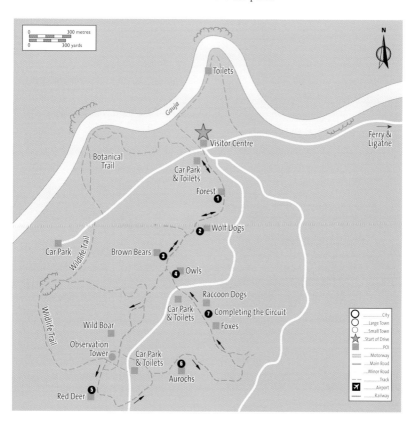

Latvian literary figures

Latvia may not have too many cultural figures who have worldwide recognition, but there are a number of seminal talents who have reflected Latvian culture through the centuries as well as had a deep influence on it.

Rūdolfs Blaumanis (1863–1908)

This renowned Latvian writer is still warmly regarded today for his ability to capture the spirit and feelings of the man on the street. His subjects tended to be modest but his writing is brilliant at times. He had a prolific output of plays, poetry and novels: two of his most celebrated plays are *The Indrans* and the comedy *A Tailor's Day in Silmeci*; his novel *Frost in Spring* is widely read in Latvia. The flat where he rented a room from 1906 until his death is now open as the Jaṇa Rozentāla un Rūdolfa Blaumaṇa Muzejs (Janis Rozentals and Rūdolfs Blaumanis Museum) (*Alberta Iela 12, Rīga; tel: 733 1641; admission charge*).

Andrējs Pumpurs (1841–1902)

Pumpurs is perhaps remembered more as a collator than as a creative writer. His speciality was to delve into Latvia's rich (often oral) folk traditions and record them for future generations to savour. He worked in the 19th century and is remembered most for *Lāčplēšis* (*The Bear Slayer*), which has become Latvia's national epic – a tale where its eponymous hero battles a German knight before meeting his tragic fate in the Daugava

The impressive Pumpurs Museum

Jānis Rainis' house

River. The German crusaders are referred to in this work as 'the beast rising up from the sea', and it is symbolic of the effort of the Latvians to avoid being crushed by the German Knights. There is an Andrejs Pumpurs Museum on the banks of the Daugava River (see p89).

Jānis Rainis (1865–1929)

Perhaps Latvia's most famous poet, Rainis started writing early; he was still a teenager when he was first heralded for his translation of Pushkin's *Boris Godunov*. He was well known both as a poet and a playwright; his most acclaimed play is *Joseph and his Brothers*. As part of the 'New Movement', he was influential in the Latvian search for a national identity: his play *I Played and Danced* is a rally-call against foreign domination. Rainis was no literary recluse. He was heavily active in political life, returning from exile to serve in the first independent Latvia in the 1920s, a period when he was also appointed director of the Latvian National Theatre. There is a museum dedicated to his work just outside Daugavpils (see p103).

Kārlis Skalbe (1879–1945)

Skalbe's achievements are often underplayed, perhaps because he worked mainly in the sphere of fairy tales. However, what on the surface may seem like innocent stories for children, at other levels delve into Latvian myths and folklore and contain allegorical depictions of the world around. Skalbe's rural cottage has now been turned into a museum (Saulrieti); his family grave, including his own tomb, is on the site (*Vecpiebalga; tel: 416 4252; admission charge*).

Krišjānis Valdemārs (1825–91)

Valdemārs, a man of letters credited with founding the first Latvian language newspaper, was one of the most famous figures associated with the 'National Awakening' in the 19th century. A prolific writer, he produced a large number of short stories and riddles, and was also heavily involved in political debate through pamphlets, letters, newspapers and other publications. Some estimates say he wrote over 10,000 letters, although only a small proportion of these survive today.

Typical wooden door in central Vidzeme

(besides various temporary exhibitions), much of which he wrote while living in the area. There are also some fine sand caves dotted in and around Liepa, which are marked on the Gauja National Park map on sale in the tourist offices in Cēsis and Sigulda.

Līgatne

This modest little village is worth a brief stop to admire its setting in the national park and its quiet ambience. Nearby is a famous ferry that takes you across the Gauja. It basically looks like a wooden pier, which divorces itself from one bank and stations itself at the other, with only a cable to help it cross. Cars are allowed on this perilous-looking device – something of a relic today, harking back to pre-independence Latvia without motorways and new bridges. A wildlife trail also starts nearby (*see pp118–19*).

Limbaži

The old provincial town of Limbaži is a good place to while away an hour or two. Once Limbaši prospered as a member of the Hanseatic League, but those days of glory are long gone. It has not been jazzed up since, like many other small towns across the country, which is not necessarily a bad thing as its old cobbled roads have not been smoothed over and its mixture of wooden and brick buildings has an unmistakable faded charm.

If you are parking in the main car park on the road in from Cēsis, look

AROUND CENTRAL VIDZEME

While the natural attractions of the Gauja National Park rightly draw all the plaudits, there is more to the Central Vidzeme region: a string of towns and villages well worth visiting on the way from the park itself right up to the Estonian border in the far north.

Liepa

Just north of Cēsis is Liepa, which is famous as the site of the grave of one of Latvia's literary lights, Eduards Veidenbaums, who died in 1892. His old house is on the outskirts of the town at Kalači, which now functions as a museum dedicated to the poet's work out for a sprightly statue welcoming you. This is Kārlis Baumanis, author of the country's national anthem, *God Bless Latvia*, which was first heard publicly in 1873 and became the national anthem upon independence in 1920. The statue itself dates from the first period of Latvian independence and did well to survive the Soviet years.

The main sights of the town include the castle and the Orthodox church. The castle overlooks a lake and has witnessed several makeovers over the centuries, from a wooden Liv fort to a sturdier Teutonic version; the impressive Orthodox church seems a little too grand for sleepy Limbaži. *Limbaži Tourist Information Centre, Burtnieku Iela 5. Tel: 6407 0608. www.limbazi.lv*

Rauna

Rauna is one of those attractive little towns you find all over Latvia, with a ruined castle mound to remind one of its past, and a pretty church. It is a pleasant place to idle around if Cēsis is busy at the height of the tourist season.

Vidzeme

The castle in Limbaži

The elegant Lutheran church, at the heart of Limbaži

Smiltene

A castle stood on the site where the town now stands as early as the 13th century, but the various wars and invaders who swept through Smiltene ensured there was little left to see of it bar its mound. More interesting is the town's Lutheran church, which claims to be the only one in the country with a crossed nave, finished in 1859; and Kalnamuiza, a museum built around an old baronial farming estate with reconstructed buildings.

Smiltene Tourist Information Centre, Dāra Iela 3. Tel: 6470 7575.
www.smiltene.lv

Strenči

This otherwise unassuming town set in one of the most charming stretches of the Gauja River Valley is famous for its annual raft festival. The skills of the local craftspeople are legendary, and these days they are put to the test at this very popular event. There is also a modest museum dedicated to the local raftsmen and the festival. The rapids lie around 3km (2 miles) down the Gauja from the town itself.

Valka

The otherwise innocuous border town of Valka is notorious for one thing – that it is only half a town, literally. What was once one town is now split between Estonia (Valga) and Latvia (Valka). Few other places in Europe offer such a geopolitical anomaly, and Valka is worth visiting for this reason alone. Ironically, even as the Soviet bloc meant division and harsh new borders for much of Eastern Europe, it actually united this town as the relatively new borders between the fledgling nations of Estonia and Latvia were demolished under rule from Moscow.

Valka Tourist Information Centre, Rīgas Iela 22. Tel: 6472 5522.
www.valka.lv

The Border

The guards at the border do not look favourably upon tourists who wish to walk from one side of the town to the other just so that they can cross between countries. Motorists have to use a separate out-of-town crossing. If you want to see both sides of the town and the border between, climb up the observation tower at the Lutheran church (*Rīgas Iela 17*).

Also worth noting are the large number of cemeteries around Valka, said to be there not because Latvians have any great desire to have Valka as their last resting place, but because the quarrelling local nationalities and ethnicities over the years refused to be buried together. In fact, one Latvian cemetery is located on the Estonian side and vice versa, and relatives of the deceased have to be issued special permits to cross. Other anomalies include an Estonian house whose external pipes and eaves lie in Latvia, and a garage that is split between the two European Union members. A map detailing the wacky route of the border can be found on the town's tourist office website: *www.valka.lv*

Valkas Novapētniecības Muzejs (Valka Regional Museum)

The Valka Regional Museum, recently opened, delves into the town's unique history, exploring the Baltics' mini-version of Cold War Berlin. It is housed in a 19th-century building built originally to house a seminary. *Rīgas Iela 64. Tel: 6472 2198. Admission charge.*

Limbaži backstreets with their typical architecture

Valmiera

While Sigulda and Cēsis get all the tourists, Vidzeme's largest town, Valmiera, once an important member of the Hanseatic League (it joined in 1365 and stayed a member until the 16th century), stands in relative obscurity further to the north towards the Estonian border. The town, situated on the Gauja River, was once a key trading hub on the road connecting Tallinn and Pskov to Rīga and the west; these days, however, the busy highway from Tallinn skirts well past Valmiera. Valmiera was established in the 13th century with a sturdy castle built in 1283 to protect the town's inhabitants. Although its landmark fortification was largely destroyed long ago and World War II badly damaged the old town (30 per cent of the town's buildings were razed to the ground), for those with time to spare in Vidzeme Valmiera is a rewarding day trip or even an overnight stay, especially as the local authorities have recently invested a lot of money in improving the town's appearance.

Valmiera Tourist Information Centre, Rīgas Iela 10. Tel: 6420 7177. www.valmiera.lv

Valmieras Pilsdrupas un Novapētniecības Muzejs (Valmiera Castle and Regional Museum)

The regional museum of Valmiera sits on the hillock where the Livonian Order castle once stood, and you can still see some of the old walls and foundations that hint at the town's grand history. The exhibits in the museum tell us of the past of Valmiera and the surrounding area. Outside the museum you can follow a trail south down to the river, a nice walk on a sunny day. The park is popular with the locals and you can walk around or sit on the benches and take in views of the Gauja as it flows through on its course to the Gauja National Park. There are cultural events in the park during the summer. Look out for the viewing point, the best place in town to take in the sweep of the river.

Brunieuku Iela 3. Tel: 422 3620. Admission charge.

Churches

A church has stood at the site of Svētā Sīmana Baznīca (St Simon's Church),

Valmiera is located beside the Gauja River

Town hall square in Valmiera

Brunieuku Iela 2, since the 13th century. The current incarnation boasts a famous 19th-century organ by F. Ladegasts. You can climb the church tower for a view of Valmiera from a height. The town's Orthodox church on Rīgas Iela is made up largely of red brick and has attractive blue onion domes.

Valmieras Drāmas Teātris (Valmiera Drama Theatre)

One of the most famous theatres in the country stands in Valmiera, just a short walk from the castle ruins. Today's building dates back to only the 1980s, but the history of the theatre goes back to the 19th century. The theatre company based here celebrated its 85th anniversary in 2004. It has travelled successfully to Russia and the USA; most of the performances in Valmiera are exclusively in Latvian, but the standards are high enough to transcend the language barrier. Valmiera is also home to the country's first music school outside Rīga, which opened in 1920.
Lāčplēsa Iela 4. Tel: 420 7335.
www.theatre.lv

The forest-shrouded shores of Lake Alūksne

Alūksne

Most visitors go to Alūksne to see its lake surrounded by lush forest; however, the town itself has a handful of interesting sights that merit spending a couple of hours' exploration.

Alūksne Tourist Information Centre, Pils Iela 74. Tel: 6432 2804. www.aluksne.lv

Alūksnes Ezers (Lake Alūksne)

This tranquil body of water, one of the biggest lakes in Latvia, is popular with local fishermen who can be spotted casting their lines from small rowing boats. You can while away a pleasant hour or so here enjoying a picnic on the banks, or indulge in a spot of angling yourself.

Alūksnes Jaunā Pils
(Alūksne New Castle)

This neo-Gothic structure, constructed at the bequest of Baron Alexander von Vietinghoff, was completed in 1863.

Formerly used by the military, today the mansion is occupied by two museums and a cinema amongst other things. The museums give an insight into local life and the region's natural surroundings, as well as commanding views over the lake.

Alūksnes Livonijas Ordeņa Pilsdrupas
(Livonian Order Castle Ruins)

A Livonian Order castle was first built on Lake Alūksne's heavily forested Maria Island (often referred to as Pils or Castle Island) in 1342. Over the years, German, Polish and Swedish forces inhabited the fortress; the Swedes blew it up during their retreat from Russian invaders. Today the ruined castle, which is accessible by a small causeway, serves as an open-air arena that can accommodate up to 3,000 people.

Alūksnes Pils Parks
(Alūksne Castle Park)

Alūksne's Castle Park, which skirts the edge of the lake, boasts a diverse collection of monuments including a granite obelisk, a small temple dedicated to the Greek wind god, Aiolos, a 19th-century pavilion constructed in preparation for a visit by Russian Tsar Alexander, and an 18th-century greenhouse.

Bībeles Muzejs (Bible Museum)

Alūksne's Bible Museum houses more than 250 bibles, prayer books and other religious books. The centrepiece of the exhibition is a facsimile edition of

Glück's New Testament, the blueprint for the first Latvian bible.
Pils Iela 25. Free admission.

Churches

The town's 18th-century Alūksnes Evaņģēliski Luteriskā Baznīca (Alūksne Evangelical Lutheran Church) is regarded as one of the most comprehensive examples of Latvia's early classicist architecture. The attractive Alūksnes Pareizticīgo Baznīca (Alūksne Orthodox Church), constructed in 1895, features characteristic onion domes.

Glück's Oaks

From 1683 until his death Alūksne was home to the German priest Ernst Glück, the first person to translate the New and Old Testaments into Latvian. On completing each project Glück planted an oak tree, and these two enormous oaks can still be seen today.

Mazbānītis Narrow-Gauge Railway

The 33km (21-mile) stretch of track that runs between Alūksne and Gulbene is the last remaining section of narrow-gauge railway tracks in Latvia. This historic route travels through picturesque scenery at a speed of just 40kph (25mph). A steam engine, which features amongst the rolling stock, sometimes pulls the train.
www.banitis.lv

Templa Kalns (Temple Hill)

A granite rotunda dating from the turn of the 19th century stands atop the hill commemorating those who gave their lives in the Northern Wars. In 1938 a Sun Bridge joined the so-called 'Temple of Glory'.

Archaeological digs have unearthed the remains of Alūksne Castle

COASTAL VIDZEME

The slice of the Vidzeme coastline that separates Rīga from the Estonian border to the north is often ignored by visitors rattling by on the bus between Rīga and Tallinn. This is a shame as it is still relatively unexplored and has a number of things to see and do.

Ainaži

Within sniffing distance of the Estonian border, Ainaži lies at the edge of no-man's land with signposts on the roads leading there declaring 'Border Area'. The town's main claim to fame is that it was the site of Latvia's first naval college, which was opened in 1864 by Krišjānis Valdemārs, known as the 'Father of Latvian Shipping'. He is celebrated as such by a statue on the waterfront in Ventspils. Although the college itself closed in the aftermath of World War I, there is a museum, which opened in the 1960s, which celebrates the history and traditions of the naval college.

www.ainazi.lv

Liepupe

Further north is the unassuming but pleasant little settlement of Liepupe, with a river that glides through the town. Little remains of the once mighty castle that used to stand here guarding this strategic spot on the Baltic trade routes, said to have once been a major Liv stronghold.

www.liepupe.lv

Beautiful rocky beaches line coastal Vidzeme on the road north towards the Estonian border

Salacgrīva

People have sought refuge in the sheltered waters around Salacgrīva and the River Salaca for centuries, and indeed there is evidence that the port was once used by the ancient Liv tribes as a base for fishing. Today it is one of Latvia's busiest ports, though not really geared towards tourism. It is a useful base point for a trip into the Randu Plavas Nature Reserve. In this reserve, made up of coastal grasses, wild flowers and sea, ornithologists and botanists alike can explore the migratory birdlife and the rare flora.

Salacgrīva Tourist Information Centre, Rīgas Iela 10a. Tel: 6404 1254. www.salacgriva.lv

Sarkanklints
(Red Cliffs)

Near the town of Tūja is a stretch of cliffs known locally as the Red Cliffs, Latvia's longest stretch of sandstone cliffs. You can walk back south from Vitrupe to Tūja, a longish route of almost 20km (12 miles) but a spectacular one along this wild and enchanting coastline awash with weird rock formations and caves. The coast here is as dramatic as anywhere on the Baltic.

Saulkrasti

Formed by the amalgamation of three villages, Pabaži, Peterupe and Neibāde, Saulkrasti is just a short journey up the coast from Rīga with 17km (11 miles) of coastline. Once a premier spa retreat, the locals say that even the Russian

Saulkrasti beach, once a popular spa, now a popular beach with Latvians

monarchs took to the waters here. Whether that is true or not, a large number of Latvians still come here in summer to relax by the sea and take in the Baltic breezes. Those culturally inclined may want to check out the house where the Latvian literary luminary Reinis Kaudzīte once lived, at *Skolas Iela 19*, which now functions as a museum.

There is a slightly bizarre **Bicycle Museum** (*Rīgas Iela 44a; www.velomuseum.tk*). The main attraction, though, is the lovely sandy beaches complete with chunky log benches where you can sit and enjoy a picnic. If you prefer somewhere a little quieter, head further north where there is less development.

Saulkrasti Tourist Information Centre, Ainazu Iela 10. Tel: 6795 2641. www.saulkrasti.lv

Superstitions

In a country whose cultural awakening was stirred by folk music and folk stories, it is perhaps not surprising that Latvians still believe in many ancient superstitions. Although they may laugh at themselves when they do it, some Latvians will still cut the bread from the fatter end, joke that there is going to be a quarrel after spilling salt, or hope that they are not the ones left sitting in a corner.

Pagan traditions

Pagan traditions and rituals originating from Latvia's rural

Latvians are careful when laying the table, following their superstitious beliefs

communities have, over time, been assimilated with the Christian calendar and modern city life; some are still observed, however, during the country's annual festivals (*see pp20–1*). Superstitions associated with midsummer on 23 and 24 June include the making and wearing of herb wreaths and decorating homes with herb leaves, which Latvians believe will bring good luck for the rest of the year. During this festival some people also look for the mythical fern which, according to local legend, produces a golden flower during Līgo (Midsummer), in the same way that people in the UK might look for a four-leaf clover.

Bonfires are a key part of the midsummer celebrations, with some younger people keeping alive the tradition of jumping over the flames, believing that it will give them a head start in the second half of the year. Burning fires are also believed to absolve sin, banish evil and bring good health.

Eating

As in many other cultures, a number of superstitions in Latvia centre on food. Some of the most widespread notions are about salt. For example,

The drama of a Latvian Fire Festival

if a dish has too much salt in it Latvians will joke that the cook is in love; there is also a belief that spilling salt will lead to an argument.

Two superstitions relate to bread. The first slice cut from a loaf is sometimes nicknamed 'the farmer's son'. According to Latvian mythology the woman who eats this will marry a farmer's son, so in some households females (albeit light-heartedly) compete for this slice of bread in the same way that some women vie to catch the bride's bouquet at a wedding. The other belief associated with eating bread is that if the loaf is sliced from the fatter end, the eldest daughter will marry first.

Traditionally, Latvians are also superstitious about where they sit at the table and about dropping cutlery. Anyone who sits in the corner risks a curse that will prevent them from getting married for seven years. If a knife is dropped on the floor then a man will visit the house; if a fork or spoon falls from the table then the guest will be female.

Weddings

Tradition and superstition dictate that a Latvian bride should wear a white wedding dress and veil, which she should keep on until midnight. At midnight her veil is removed and given to a younger sister, an act that indicates that she will be the next daughter to marry. With this exchange the bride becomes a wife, and women replace their veils with a married woman's cap.

Getting away from it all

In the height of summer the endless procession of tour groups trawling through Latvia's historic old towns and the traffic-congested city streets could wear you down. The coastal resorts of Jūrmala and the southern stretch of Vidzeme's Baltic Coastline can also get very crowded in July and August. Nevertheless, if what you are craving is a bit of solitude, a secluded stretch of beach, a sleepy rural village, a peaceful forest walk or a stunning nature park, then these are never too far away, whatever the season.

Bicycle trails

Outside its towns and cities, Latvia's roads are surprisingly quiet; even when you are on a main highway with a designated speed limit of 90kph (56mph), there may be nobody else around. (The highways leading into Rīga and, increasingly, into other cities, are always busy; cycling on these is not recommended.) The light traffic combined with the flat lie of the land in rural areas means that you can cycle in relative peace and cover a lot of ground in a single day. More experienced cyclists may want to plan their own tour of the country; however, if you prefer the security of a group, then Rīga-based **Baltic Country Holidays** (*www.celotajs.lv*) can help you organise a cycling trip. They can also send you a cycling map detailing 67 routes across Latvia. The Manchester-based **Baltic Holidays** (*www.balticholidays.com*) is another travel agency that organises bike holidays in Latvia.

The number of agencies offering bicycle hire in Latvia is increasing; however, outside main tourist towns and key national parks or nature reserves, it may not be easy to find a rental company.

Cycling in Kurzeme

Kuldīga Tourism Information Centre (*Baznīcas Iela 5; tel: 6332 2259*) produces detailed route maps for three circular trails. The shortest is the 18km (11-mile) trail that cuts through the heart of Riežupe Nature Park with its river and underground sand caves, and the attractive Venta Valley. Another route (24km/15 miles) takes you from the old town to the Sauleskalni Arboretum via Pelči Castle. The 69km (43-mile) return journey to Alsunga is an epic bicycle ride that takes in ruined castles, traditional villages and vast swathes of unspoilt countryside.

In nearby Aizpute (*see p61*), whose cluster of wooden buildings has secured it a place on the European Cultural Heritage Listing, another bicycle trail begins. This route – Little Kurzeme Cycling Circle – covers 60km (37 miles) and takes cyclists to Kazdanga Castle, Valtaiķi Church and the Bojas Estate and Forest Museum, through fertile countryside. More information about this route is available from the Liepāja Tourism Information Centre.

Liepāja Tourism Information Centre: Rožu Laukums 5–6. Tel: 6348 0808. www.liepaja.lv

Cycling in Vidzeme

The Vidzeme Tourism Association recommends over a dozen cycle routes which can take from 4 hours (15km/ 9 miles) to 2 days (80km/50 miles). The Alūksne–Hānja Highland Route is the longest, taking in castle mounds, underground bunkers and seven lakes – if you are planning to complete the whole route you will need your passport as it crosses into Estonia. For information about this route, contact the Tourism Information Centre in Veclaicene (*tel: 6436 6160*).

Other routes run from Cēsis or Valmiera, taking in cliffs, the Gauja River valley, fresh water springs, caves and unspoilt countryside. If you have a penchant for Latvian beer, the Live Beer Route from Valmiera takes in the Brenguļi Brewery. For details about these routes and bicycle hire contact the tourist offices in Valmiera or Cēsis, who rent bicycles by the hour or by the day.

Eži Tourism Centre: Valdemāra Iela 1, Valmiera. Tel: 6420 7263. www.ezi.lv.

A cyclist exploring Latvia's bountiful countryside

Getting away from it all

Cēsis Tourist Information Centre:
Pils Laukums 1, Cēsis.
Tel: 6412 1815. www.tourism.cesis.lv

Birdwatching

Latvia is a key transit point for thousands of birds as they migrate north in the spring and south in the autumn. Its national parks and nature reserves are ideal places for watching nesting birds from March through to early summer, with Lake Kanieris in Ķemeri National Park (*see pp52–3*), Lake Engure (*see p54*) and the the Teiči and Pelecares bogs in the Teiči Nature Reserve all finding their way into the Ramsar list of Wetlands of International Importance in 1995.

Soviet rule may have stunted Latvia's economic and industrial development, but it also ensured that vast areas of wetland (due to the absence of development witnessed in most Western European countries), rich with fish stocks, were left untouched. With their precious habitat left intact, storks, geese and other migrating birds flock to the country every year. Seemingly oblivious to the great opportunities for birdwatching in their own country, very few Latvians are keen ornithologists, which means that visitors may well have the luxury of viewing rare bird species alone.

Ķemeri National Park, Kurzeme

This warren of forests and marshy bogs is a haven for nesting birds, with the bogs supporting nesting wood sandpipers, plovers, grey shrikes,

Latvia is a haven for keen birdwatchers

curlews and cranes. At Ķemeri's most important lakes, Kanieris and Skolas, which were once sea lagoons, you can commonly see waterfowl (widgeon, goldeneye, goosander and ducks) and geese; eagles and ospreys have been known to feed here too. The park's meadows are important nesting ground for corncrakes and reed warblers, while various species of woodpecker and black storks choose to nest in the forest. If you are lucky you might even see white-tailed eagles, lesser-spotted eagles and owls (eagle and pygmy) that also nest here. If your birdwatching does not go according to plan, you can always take a trip to Ķemeri's beaches where you are almost guaranteed to spot seabirds (*see pp52–3*).

Lake Engure Nature Park, Kurzeme

This large freshwater lake supports more than 170 types of nesting birds – including around 40 threatened or endangered species – and more than 800 types of flora. During the breeding season over 20,000 waterfowl can also be found here. Various species of ducks, grebes and swans can be spotted from the birdwatching towers on the northern, eastern and western shores of Lake Engure. Lucky visitors might also see white-tailed eagles, corncrakes, white storks, black storks, spotted harriers, marsh crakes and cranes, to name just a few species. Contact the

WILD HORSES OF PAPE

During the Middle Ages a large number of Tarpans (European wild horses) thrived in the Baltic countries. By the beginning of the 20th century these horses had been overhunted and their feeding grounds were erased, making them almost extinct. In 1936 wild horses were discovered in Poland, and these animals were reintroduced to Latvia in 1999. In 2006 there were 30 Tarpans in Pape National Park. Protected by the World Wide Fund for Nature (WWF), the horses can only be viewed with a guide (*see pp76–7*).

lake's ornithological centre (*Bērzciems. Tel: 2947 4420. www.eedp.lv*) for more information.

Āraiši Lake is another ideal getting-away spot

Getting away from it all

The Gauja is Latvia's longest river

Lake Pape

While most people come to the Pape Nature Reserve to view its wild horses (*see pp76–7*), it is also a great birdwatching spot; over 270 species of birds can be viewed from the park's towers. The birds that nest, feed or breed here include grey herons, black kites, red kites, buzzards, golden eagle and kestrel, alongside various species of waterfowl.
www.pdf-pape.lv

Lubana Wetlands

Located in the Latgale region of the country, Latvia's largest wetland area incorporates Latvia's largest lake (*see pp98–9*), and is a thriving nesting and breeding ground for many species of birds including swans, pintails, terns, woodpeckers and various types of eagle. The most commonly spotted birds from its four viewing towers are migrating swans, geese and ducks.

Teiči Nature Reserve, Vidzeme

The Teiči and Pelecares bogs constitute the largest mossy bog in the Baltics, dating back some 10,000 years, and are home to a thriving community of rare and endangered birds, many of which stop here on their migration routes. Black storks, black-throated loons, cliff eagles, grey herons, marsh sandpipers, small eagles and yellow plovers are just some of the birds that can be spotted here. The ecology of the park is so precious that access is granted only if

you are accompanied by an official guide, so it is never too crowded.
Aiviekstes 3, Ļaudona.
Tel: 6480 7206. www.teici.gov.lv

Canoeing/Kayaking

Many of Latvia's rivers and lakes are perfect for a tranquil canoe trip, with kayaks, canoes and small rowing boats available for hire during the summer in many locations. A short trip on Lake Engure (*see p54*) can help remove the stresses of city life, but to really get away from it all, undertake a longer journey with overnight camping.

Vidzeme's inland waterways

With a course that flows 452km (281 miles), the Gauja is Latvia's longest river and the quintessential destination for canoeists. If you have your own kayak or a hired one, choose how long you want to spend on the river; alternatively, join a small group and cover from 9 to 137km (5 1/2 to 85 miles) in a half-day or five-day journey. One of the most scenic stretches of the river lies between Cēsis and Sigulda and takes two to three days to cover (*see p116*).

Deserted beaches

During the summer months the Vidzeme coastline just north of Rīga and the Jūrmala Baltic Sea coast, both easily accessible from the capital, are bustling holiday spots. Yet many visitors (and Latvians) forget that the country's coastline measures nearly

500km (310 miles) – the majority of which is deserted at any time of year. After you have found a tranquil stretch of sand, you can always scour the beach for fragments of amber.

Fishing

Fishing is a popular sport in Latvia, with an annual fly-fishing championship held every September – the location varies, but past competitions have been held in Rīga and on the Gauja River. As winter closes in, the anglers continue undeterred, turning their hand to ice fishing instead; this too has an annual competition of its own – the CIPS Ice Fishing World Championship. In a country that has more than 2,000 lakes and around 12,500 rivers you don't have to be a serious angler to enjoy fishing. The country's largest lakes, Lubans, Ražna and Engure, and its longest rivers, the Daugava, Lielupe, Venta, Aviiekste and Gauja, are all obvious places to cast a line, and it is never too hard to find a secluded spot. Locals take a more relaxed approach to fishing, simply parking their cars next to a lake, stream or river and casting a net or line, even in towns like Talsi. In the summer, deep-sea fishing on Latvia's Baltic Sea coast is another option.

Basics

If you are planning to fish in Latvia, there are a few basics that you need to know. The country's inland waters are home to 42 species of fish and three

A lovely stretch of the Jūrmala coast surrounded by towering pine trees

species of lamprey, with bream, carp, loach, perch, pike, roach, trench and white bream commonly seen in rivers and lakes. Salmon can also be caught in the rivers, while sea trout, salmon, lamprey and crustaceans populate the sea.

In 1997 the Latvian government introduced a new law which specified that anglers need a permit or angling card to fish in state-owned waters. However, many Latvians disregard this and the law is not very strictly enforced. You also need to secure permission to fish on private land. The local tourist office will be able to advise you about fishing rights in a particular area.

While law enforcement of fishing permits may be lax, the regulations about what you are or are not allowed to catch are not. As a rule of thumb, anglers cannot fish for lamprey, sea trout or salmon from the Baltic unless they have a licence to do so. In fresh water pike fishing is off limits from mid-March to the end of April, perch fishing is prohibited in May, and brown trout cannot be caught in October and November.

Hiking

You will not find any challenging ascents in this largely pancake-flat country; however, Latvia's lush natural environment of forests, lakes and rivers still invites exploration on foot. Well-signposted woodland trails dot the country's national parks and nature reserves; you can also pick pathways up in any of the forested areas. Woodland hiking may be rewarded by sightings of numerous bird species, roe deer, elk, wild boar, bears or even lynx. The forest flora is also diverse and includes orchids, summer berries and fungi (while it is perfectly acceptable to pick fruits that you find growing in the forest, you should do this only if you are absolutely certain about what they are).

If you intend to do serious walking, tourist offices and associations throughout the country will be able to suggest routes. If you want to learn

RURAL ESCAPES

The concept of rural tourism is relatively new in Latvia, and while an increasing number of people rent out spare rooms or custom-built log cabins, accommodation can be hard to organise without a bit of help. Baltic Country Holidays is an agency with multilingual staff that can help you book your rural retreat in advance without charging you a fee (this is absorbed by the provider). In 2007 it had over 300 members throughout Latvia, a figure that is set to rise.

Lauku Celotajs (Latvian Country Tourism Association): Kugu Iela 11, Rīga. Tel: 6761 7600. www.celotajs.lv

more about the wildlife and plants that you will see on your way, hire a local guide. This can also be arranged through tourist offices, but will generally require some notice.

Once extinct in Latvia, the brown bear can now be seen on a Līgatne Nature Trail walk

Getting away from it all

142

Getting away from it all

Hiking in Vidzeme

With more than 20 routes – taking between 2 hours (1.3km/³/₄ mile) to a whole day (15km/9 miles) – identified by the Vidzeme Tourism Association alone, you are literally spoilt for choice in this region. The Eži Tourism Centre in Valmiera (*see p135*) can give you details about a walk around Vaidava Lake or the cliffs and caves on the Striķupe Trail. Alternatively, explore the Cīrulīši Nature Trail near Cēsis. Other popular walks in Vidzeme take you deep into the forested Līgatne Nature Park (*see pp118–19*) and Gauja National Park (*see pp112–19*).

National Parks and Nature Reserves

Latvians are passionate about their natural environment, and the country has around 500 national parks and nature reserves. At weekends and during holidays people leave the city in droves so that they can be closer to nature. Fortunately, such a large proportion of the country offers unspoilt rural landscapes, lush forests and pristine sands that these oases rarely feel overcrowded. In fact, you may well find yourself completely on your own as you walk through a forest, kayak on a river, fish in a lake or stroll

Striking cliffs are a feature of Gauja National Park

along a beach. One of the best ways for visitors to learn about the Latvian countryside and coastline, as well as its fauna and flora, is to visit some of its National Parks and Nature Reserves. The Nature Protection Board safeguards Latvia's natural heritage. *Eksporta Iela 5, Rīga.*
Tel: 6750 9545. www.dap.gov.lv

Gauja National Park, Vidzeme

You can literally lose yourself in Latvia's oldest national park (*see pp112–19*).

Ķemeri National Park, Kurzeme

Numerous walking trails run through Ķemeri's dense pine forests and you will always be able to find a secluded path. Latvians seeking solitude tend to jump off the bus when they see a walkway leading into the forest, or simply abandon their cars on one of the many dirt tracks that run through the reserve (*see pp52–3*).

Lake Engure Nature Park, Kurzeme

The park's authorities strictly regulate recreation on this large lagoon-type lake, but they will grant permission to fish and rent small rowing boats from four locations (Krievragciems, Dzedri, Mazsaliņa and Briežragi). For those not intending to take to the water, one of the most enjoyable and relaxing activities is to follow the 3.5km (2$^1\!/_4$-mile) orchid trail, where you can view 22 of the 32 orchid species native to Latvia (*see p54*).
Bērciems. Tel: 2947 4420. www.eedp.lv

North Vidzeme Biosphere Reserve, Vidzeme

This diverse nature park boasts 60km (37 miles) of coastline, complete with sandy beaches and sandstone outcrops unique to the area, and one of the most expansive marshes in the Baltic region. It is also home to the largest salmon spawning area along the Baltic Sea coast, on the Salaca River.

The large coastal plains inside the reserve are home to over 650 indigenous species of plants; they are also an important stopping point on the migratory route of geese, cranes and white storks.
Rīgas Iela 10a, Salacgrīva.
Tel: 6407 1408. www.biosfera.lv

Slītere National Park, Kurzeme

Sand dunes, peat bogs and berry yews (coniferous pines) form part of Slītere's impressive landscape, some of which dates back over 11,000 years. In the park you can follow a coastal trail to watch the Baltic Sea and the Gulf of Rīga crash into one another at Cape Kolka, or admire the vista from Slītere Lighthouse (*see p63*).

If you book a guide you can also explore the delicate ecosystem of swamp and forest behind the lighthouse, where you may be lucky enough to spot badgers, beavers, black storks or green woodpeckers.
Park Administration:
Dakterlejas 3, Dundaga. Tel: 6329 1066.
www.slitere.gov.lv

Shopping

Less than two decades ago Latvia was a country that endured Soviet-era privations and food queues. These days this go-getting nation is catching up fast, with air-conditioned malls springing up in its cities and the ubiquitous supermarket adding convenience, but threatening small stores nationwide. Thankfully there are still plenty of characterful places to buy souvenirs, such as markets and souvenir stalls in the cities. It is not exactly Milan, but you will find most things that you need in Latvia, as well as a few surprises.

TAX-FREE SHOPPING

If your return flight is to a non-EU country, you can claim a tax refund at the airport. Shops offering tax-free shopping display 'Tax-Free' stickers and will issue a Global Refund cheque at the time of purchase. To be eligible for a refund each individual purchase must have been over Ls 29.50, the original receipt must be retained and goods

Amber jewellery on sale in Rīga

should not have been unwrapped. After the customs officials have stamped your 'Tax-Free' cheques, claim the refund at the pay office.

WHAT TO BUY
Amber

Around 80 per cent of the world's amber comes from the Baltic Sea area, and you can buy some stunning pieces of jewellery in Latvia. If you are going to part with a large sum of money, ask to see a certificate showing that the amber is authentic (*see pp56–7*).

Antiques

Many of Latvia's precious antiques were destroyed under Soviet occupation, so you are more likely to pick up interesting knick-knacks than anything of real value in the country's antique stores. The antique shops, though, are great places to learn about the country and to find some truly unique souvenirs: figurines in traditional

Grass Market in Rīga

Latvian costume, retro lamps or inexpensive paintings, for instance.

Beer

With so many varieties of Latvian beer on sale, your luggage will probably be too heavy if you try to take them all home as souvenirs. A few bottles of your favourite brew should go down nicely, though, as you recall your travels once you are back home (*see pp166–7*).

Ceramics

Latvians are proud of their craft traditions, with ceramic plates, bowls, jugs and mugs having been produced in the country for centuries. Decorative mugs with images of rural life or city scenes, as well as modern creations, make good gifts. Pick up more traditional pieces from antique shops.

Confectionery

After you have tasted the handmade chocolates of Emihla Gustava Schokolahde (*www.sokolade.lv*), you will not want to go back to anything else. If your budget does not stretch to luxury chocolates the manufactured Laima brand is also delicious.

Folk music

Folk music is an integral part of Latvian culture (*see p19*) and prominent in many festivals and events. You can take home your own slice of Latvian culture in the form of a music CD.

Linen/lace and woollen items

Hand-woven garments, rugs and intricate lace items are available as souvenirs.

Craft market, Kuldīga

Rīga Melnais Balzams (Rīga Black Balsams)

Worth buying as much for its distinctive ceramic bottle as for the novelty value of gifting friends and family with a potent alcoholic drink. Once the contents of the bottle have been emptied, you can copy the bar at Torņa Iela 4 (*see p148*) and turn it into a stylish oil burner.

Toiletries and cosmetics

If you are shopping in Rīga, look out for excellent soaps, aromatherapy oils and bath salts produced by Stendera Ziepju Fabrika (Stender's Soap Factory).

WHERE TO SHOP

Rīga is the best place to shop in Latvia.

Rīga

Art Nouveau Rīga

Exclusive gifts and souvenirs in the Art Nouveau or Jugendstil design for which the city is famous.
Strēlnieku Iela 9. Tel: 733 3030.

Emihla Gustava Schokolahde

Selling wonderfully rich chocolates of the same name. They'll even gift-wrap your purchases.
Marijas 13/U1 (Berga bazārs).

Dzintars

The name may mean amber, but the goods on sale are definitely not. Pick up cosmetics, hair products and gifts from the 'Misters' range. Your friends will no doubt be impressed when you tell them this brand was very popular with the Soviets when Latvia was part of the USSR.
Grēcinieku Iela 22-24. Tel: 762 1625.

Suvenīru Studija

A great little old-town souvenir shop selling wooden, woollen, leather and ceramic goods.
Kaļķu Iela 20.

UPE

Ornate and attractive musical instruments make unusual souvenirs, while there are traditional toys for younger friends and relatives.
Vāgnera Iela 5. Tel: 6722 6119.

Jūrmala

The shops in Majori may seem a little run-down, but you can still find some decent souvenirs.

Antikvariāta

If you did not find any Latvian antiques in Rīga, try your luck at this shop.
Jomas Iela 56.

Londa

For forgotten toiletries or cosmetics head to Londa, with its large choice of products.
Jomas Iela 66. Tel: 776 1243.

Pie Mestra

Join your fellow tourists in souvenir shopping.
Jomas Iela 85.

Sporta Veikals

If you have forgotten any of your outdoor or sports gear, this place is where you are likely to get these.
Jomas Iela 40.

Kuldīga
Juvelieris

Check out the ancient building in the same block as the old town hall, as much of the jewellery is on offer.
Pastas Iela.

Suvenīri Artar

Ignore the usually cool reception and step inside to check out smaller woollen and lace items.
Baznīcas Iela 5.

Weavers' Workshop

Intricately patterned hand-woven rugs entice shoppers in from the street.
Baznīcas Iela 5.

Liepāja
Lauma

Formerly a favourite with ladies from the USSR, the Lauma underwear factory in Liepāja is still going strong. A great place to pick up elegant lingerie at good prices.
Liela Iela 12. Tel: 344 1091.

MARKETS

Latvian markets are not geared for visitors, selling mainly cheap clothing and fresh food. If you are self-catering, shopping in a market could save you a lot of money. The market can also be a lot of fun for an idle wander.

Centrāltirgus (Rīga Central Market)

This large market sells a wide range of goods including hardware and food. One of the nicest things about visiting it is walking past the brightly coloured flower stalls. If you need to pick up an item of clothing but don't want to spend a fortune, this is a good place to come (*see p30*).

Jūrmala

The bustling markets in Buldurin, Dubulti and Kauguri are great places to wander around. In summer you may be able to pick up a few souvenirs alongside the usual foodstuff and fresh produce.

Liepāja

Foodstuffs are the main item on sale here, but it is also a good place to pick up honey, edible seeds, or to simply absorb a different pace of life; it feels like the clocks have been turned back 40 years in the market hall (*see p75*).

Entertainment

Rīga's Old Town is crammed with a diverse range of bars and cafés, with everything from lounge-style hangouts to dives that seem stuck in a time warp. Rīga has also recently taken on the somewhat dubious role of one of Europe's 'sex capitals', but this type of establishment is easily avoided.

RĪGA
Ballet
Rīga Ballet

The quality of Latvia's ballet is a legacy of the Soviet days, with the ballet school held in the same high regard as the Kirov and Bolshoi ballets (*see p18*). *Various venues. Check at the Tourist Information Centre (see p33).*

Bars
De Lacy's

A new contender for the best pint of Guinness in the city. An immediate

Enjoying a sunset drink in the Skyline Bar

favourite with both expats and locals looking to meet native English-language speakers.
Skūņu Iela 4.

Orange

Pumping out alternative tunes, this bar, with an orange colour scheme, attracts a young and lively crowd.
Jāņa Iela 5. Tel: 6722 8423.

Rīgas Balzams

If its name doesn't give it away, Rīga Melnais Balzams (*see pp40–1*) bottles doubling up as candles and an extensive cocktail list featuring the potent alcohol leave you in no doubt what this lively bar is all about.
Torņa Iela 4. Tel: 6721 4494.

The Skyline Bar

Table service, relaxing music and fine cocktails complement the superb views from the 26th floor of the Reval Hotel Latvija.
Elizabetes Iela 55. Tel: 6777 2222.

Latvian Theatre

Blues and jazz music
Bites Blues Club
When there is no live show the club plays classic jazz on a large screen.
Dzirnavu Iela 34a.
Tel: 6733 3123. www.bluesclub.lv

Hamlet Club
Modern jazz in arty surrounds.
Jana Seta Iela 5. Tel: 6722 9938.

Casinos
Rīga's casinos are not all above-board, so it is best to stick to reputable ones like those located in 5-star hotels:

Olympic Casino
You'll need photographic ID to register.
Kuagu 24 (Radisson SAS).
Open 24 hours.

Cinema
Films are often screened with the original language audible below the Latvian dubbing. Look out for original-language versions if you are planning a trip to the cinema.

Coca-Cola Plaza
Don't forget to pop up to the Parex Forum bar for great city views.
Janvara Iela 8, Rīga.
www.forumcinemas.lv

The Daile Cinema
Barona 31, Rīga. www.forumcinemas.lv

Circus
Rīga is the only Latvian city to have a permanent circus. Its performance schedule is available on its website.
Merkela 4. Tel: 6721 3279. www.cirks.lv

Classical music
Latvian National Symphony Orchestra
Latvia's first-rate symphony orchestra is based in Rīga's Guildhall.
Amatu Iela 6. Tel: 6721 3798.

Wagner Hall
A great place to catch a smaller concert.
Vāgnera Iela 4. Tel: 6722 7105.

Opera
Latvian National Opera
Latvia's excellent opera company is finally back where it belongs, in the reconstructed Rīga Opera House.
Aspazijas Bulvāris 3.
Tel: 6707 3777. www.opera.lv

Nightclubs
Depo
This underground hangout has an alternative buzz. Keep your eyes peeled for flyers promoting guest DJs.
Vaļņu Iela 32. Tel: 6722 0114.

La Rocca

Rīga's largest club hosts a variety of club nights that cater to all kinds of music. A youthful crowd and affordable drinks make this a popular choice.
Brīvības Iela 96. Tel: 6750 6030.

Nautilus

The décor at this quirky club has a submarine theme and the bar staff dress in sailor suits.
Kungu Iela 8. Tel: 6781 4455.

Nobody Writes to the Colonel

This grunge-style bar is a perennial favourite with the trendy set in Rīga. It also often functions as a bustling club that veers towards alternative music. Downstairs is more fun and funky.
Peldu Iela 26/28.
Tel: 6721 3886.

Theatre

Rīga has the best theatres in the country, with its productions often more cutting-edge than those staged elsewhere in Latvia. The city's main theatres are listed below:

Dailes Theatre

Brīvības Iela 75.
Tel: 727 9566. www.dailesteatris.lv

Krievu Dramas Teatris
(Russian Drama Theatre)

Kalku Iela 16. Tel: 6722 5395.
www.trd.lv

Nacionalais Teatris
(National Theatre)

Kronvalda Bulvāris 2.
Tel: 6700 6302. www.teatris.lv

Rīgas Jaunais Teatris
(New Rīga Theatre)

Lacplesa Iela 25. Tel: 728 0765.
www.jrt.lv

Jūrmala
Casino Olympic

This casino, adjacent to the Hotel Jūrmala Spa, is open 24 hours.
Jomas Iela 47/49. Tel: 6776 4433.

Majori Culture House and Cinema

Doubles up as an exhibition area, concert venue, cinema and jazz club.
Jomas Iela 35. Tel: 6776 2403.

Salmu Krogs

This traditionally styled bar with a thatched roof and a buzzing outdoor seating area during summer is a great place to sample Latvian beers.
Jomas Iela 70. Tel: 776 1393.

Seaside

The 11th-floor bar of the Hotel Jūrmala Spa boasts a stylish interior, good cocktails and great Baltic Sea views.
Jomas Iela 47/49. Tel: 6778 4420.

Slavu

The second floor of this centrally located restaurant doubles up as a club at weekends and during the summer.
Jomas Iela 57. Tel: 6776 1401.

KURZEME
Ventspils
Kurzeme

Don't make the mistake of judging this place by its exterior. The complex boasts a cosy coffee shop, an attractive restaurant and a stylish bar. There is even a dance floor, making it one of the liveliest places in the Old Town.
Jūras Iela 8. Tel: 6362 4158.

Livonija

This restaurant-bar-nightclub has comfy leather sofas and cheap beer.
Talsu Iela 8. Tel: 6362 2287.

VIDZEME
Cēsis
Hotel Kolonna Cēsis

The hotel's summer terrace and bistro-bar are the liveliest spots in town.
Vienības Laukums 1. Tel: 6412 0122.

Pils Park (Castle Park)

During the summer, concerts are performed in the attractive open-air setting of Pils Park, with the castle ruins rearing up behind the stage. Look out for flyers and ask at the tourist office about performances.

Sigulda
Melnais Kakis (Black Cat)

This complex includes a hotel, café, restaurant, terrace and games room with electronic gambling machines. In season this is the liveliest place in town.
Pils Iela 8. Tel: 2915 0104.

Valmiera
Akācija

A busy bar serving cheap Latvian food.
Rīgas Iela 10. Tel: 423 3812.

ZEMGALE
Jelgava
Multi-Klubs

This busy nightclub opens its doors until well into the early hours.
Tirgu Iela 5.

Zemgale Recreation Centre

The ten-pin bowling alley and bar at this entertainment complex make it one of the liveliest places in Jelgava.
Rīgas Iela 11.

Rīga Opera House is a hub of the city's cultural life

Children

Despite being such a small country, Latvia offers a surprising number of activities for families with children. Fun-filled hours can be spent on Blue Flag beaches, exploring nature parks, or checking out ruined castles. On rainy or winter days families can occupy their time ten-pin bowling (see p158) or exploring one of the country's museums. Latvia is also a great place for outdoor pursuits like cycling, walking and canoeing (see p134–43).

Rīga

Latvijas Etnogrāfiskais Brīvības Muzejs (Latvian Ethnographic Museum)

Situated on the outskirts of the city, the ethnographic museum is both educational and enjoyable, allowing kids to explore old Latvian dwellings, a fisherman's village, farmhouses, churches and an old windmill. At weekends the place is brought to life by actors in period costume taking on the roles of weavers, blacksmiths and other craftspeople (*see p44*).

Lido Recreation Centre

Two floors of Latvian cuisine, a brewery, live music and a host of children's activities, including roller-skating and ice-skating, means that the Lido has something on offer for every member of the family.

Cycling in Ķemeri National Park

Krasta Iela 76. Tel: 6750 4420.
http://ac.lido.lv. Free admission.

Rīgas Motormuzejs
(Rīga Motor Museum)

The biggest automobile museum in the Baltic states gives kids and adults alike the chance to get behind the wheel of antique vehicles; you can also pose for a photo in an armoured vehicle or a 1912 fire engine (*see pp44–5*).

Rīga's parks

Rīga has a wealth of parks, of which Mežaparks and Esplanāde are particularly good for children. In the expansive Mežaparks join the locals as they walk, rollerblade or cycle around the Kīšezers Lakes (in season skates and bicycles can be hired at the park). The Esplanāde's trampolines and miniature motorised cars are great attractions for the younger ones, while the beer garden and stunning Orthodox cathedral are strictly for adults. For more information on Rīga's parks, see pp42–3.

Rīgas Zoodārzs (Rīga National Zoo)

While away a pleasant hour or two visiting the park's 475 species of animals, including elephants, polar bears, camels, ostriches, tigers and Galapagos tortoises. Located in the leafy Mežaparks (Forest Park), Rīga's zoo is reasonably well run; pony rides and horse-drawn carriages are an added bonus.
Meža prospects 1. Tel: 751 8669; www.rigazoo.lv. Admission charge.

Activities Outside Rīga
Līvu Akvaparks (Aqua Park)

Northern Europe's largest water park has six slides, a wave pool and rapids for tubing – enough to keep children happy and wet all day. Parts of the aqua park are open all year round.
Viestura Iela 24, Jūrmala. Tel: 6775 5636. www.akvaparks.lv. Admission charge.

Beaches

Equipped with a bucket and spade, children can keep themselves occupied for hours on pristine stretches of white sand. The busy resort beaches of Majori in Jūrmala are equipped for families, with beach cafés, changing facilities, restaurants and children's playgrounds.

Alternatively, drive further down the Jūrmala coast road and select a secluded spot of sand backed by dunes and pine trees – Ragaciems, Klapkalnciems and Apšuciems all have good beaches. The cities of Ventspils, Liepāja, Daughupils have Blue Flag beaches.

Castle ruins

Most children love wandering around castle ruins, imagining that they are knights from the past attacking the castle's defences. There is an intriguing range of fortresses to explore in Latvia – from the wooden fort at Lielevārde (*see pp88–9*) and the spectacular ruins at Bauska (*see p82*) and Ludza (*see p96*) to the reconstructed giant in the Turaida Reserve (*see p115*).

Exploring the coast at Rīga

Cīruļi (Kalvenes Zoo)

Don't come here expecting to see big animals like lions, tigers, zebras and elephants; instead, Cīruļi gives young and old visitors alike the chance to see some of Latvia's shyest wild animals, like wild boars, brown bears and lynxes. The zoo has a petting area and stages bird shows (*Sat–Sun afternoons*).
Near Liepāja. Contact Liepāja Tourist Information Centre for more details (see p72). Open: Apr–Oct. Admission charge.

Coastline

The windswept beaches along the Kurzeme and Vidzeme coastlines are great for a bracing walk. At Cape Kolka, if the weather is right, children can marvel at the sight of the Gulf of Rīga and the Baltic Sea slamming into one another (*see p63*).

Liepāja

Latvia's third-biggest city is a winner with children, who love its pristine Blue Flag beach and the leafy seaside park. Stretching along the coast for 3km (2 miles), the park comes complete with tennis courts, a mini golf course and a bowling club. Select your spot of sand or stretch of park, and you can watch your children play from the comfort of a beachside café.

National Parks and Nature Parks

Kurzeme's nature parks are a great place for cycling, walking and canoeing. Here children can also learn about Latvia's plants and animals. In Ķemeri

National Park go across peat bogs on raised wooden walkways as you look out for wild birds (*see pp52–3*). You can spot aurochs, bison and Latvian wild horses as you walk, cycle or sail in Pape National Park (*see pp76–7*).

In the Laumas Nature Park, close to Talsi, a variety of trails takes you on a journey where you can learn about the area's birds, plants, bees and trees. Alternatively, you can take the children fishing, take in a round of mini-golf, or hire bicycles and go on a family bike ride.

In Vidzeme, one of the biggest attractions for families is the Gauja National Park, where the riverside paths are great for cycling and horse riding. Older children can try their hand at canoeing, while younger children can share a dugout canoe with older siblings or their parents (*see pp112–19*).
Laumas Nature Park.
Tel: 640 3240. www.laumas.lv.
Admission charge.

Narrow-gauge railway
Passing through attractive countryside, the ride on Latvia's last stretch of narrow-gauge railway, which travels between Alūksne and Gulbene (*see p129*), is a real treat, especially if there happens to be a steam engine pulling the train.

Ventspils
Ventspils has both an aqua park (*see p68*) and a children's playground. In the playground 40 different activity centres and a children's café help ease the stress and strain of travelling as a family.
Playground: Lielas prospekts, Poruka.

Near Cape Kolka, Slītere National Park

Sport and leisure

Latvia offers myriad sporting activities for visitors; some are best undertaken outdoors and are dependent on the season, while others are available at indoor venues. The best months for warm-weather activities are April to September. Make sure you drink plenty of water if you are indulging in physical exercise and, where applicable, book activities in advance.

RELAXATION
Sauna and spas

The Nordic tradition of taking a sauna and then jumping into a freezing cold lake is firmly entrenched in Latvian culture, and why not – there are over 2,000 lakes to plunge into, after all. Many guesthouses, rural farm accommodation and hotels have saunas that guests can use. You will also find sauna centres in most towns and cities. Spa centres are also becoming increasingly popular (*see pp50–1*).

PARTICIPATORY SPORTS
Billiards

Billiards is a hugely popular Latvian pastime. Tables are usually available in bars and pool halls, both environments that are generally licensed and choked with cigarette smoke, and so not very child-friendly.

Cycling

This largely flat country is perfect for cycle tours, and the country's nature parks have lots of trails (*see pp134–6*). It is possible to rent bikes in the town centres and at nature parks. The local tourist office should be able to provide you with a list of places to hire bikes and suggest cycling routes. Options include:

Cēsis Tourist Information Centre
Pils Laukums 1, Cēsis. Tel: 6412 1815. www.tourism.cesis.lv

Eži Tourism Centre
Valdemāra Iela 1, Valmiera. Tel: 6420 7263. www.ezi.lv

Gandrs
Kalnciema Iela 28, Riga. Tel: 761 4775. www.gandrs.lv

Golf

Golf is still in its infancy in Latvia, but if you are keen to take in a round or two, there are a couple of decent courses located close to the capital, including Latvia's first 18-hole golf course, the Ozo Golf Club, which is located on the shores of the Kīšezers lake.

Golfs Viesturi

Viesturi Iela 1, Jaunmārupe.
Tel: 2644 4390. www.golfviesturi.lv

Ozo Golf Club

Milgrāvia Iela 16, Riga.
Tel: 6739 4399. www.ozogolf.lv

Horse riding

In a country where it is not unusual to
see a horse pulling a cart or plough in
poorer rural areas, it is perhaps
unsurprising that Latvians hold these
animals in high esteem. Horse riding is
popular in every region of Latvia, with
over 20 different opportunities for
riding in Vidzeme alone. **Burtnieku
Zirgaudzētava** (*www.burtnieki.com*) is a
web-savvy stable in Valmiera, as is
Klajumi (*www.klajumi.lv*) who organise
treks in Daugavas Loki.

Paintball

This fun and fast-paced game, which
basically involves shooting your
opponents with paint balls, is growing
in popularity in Latvia, and is sure to
be a hit with visiting stag parties. For
paintballing close to the capital, check
out the Latvian Paintball Club's website
or call Peintbols.

Latvian Paintball Club

Kr. Valdemāra 40, Rīga.
Tel: 6729 1400. www.paintball.lv

Peintbols

Priekuļu pag, near Cēsis.
Tel: 2922 4589.

Tennis

Tennis courts tend to be located in large
sports complexes; there are also courts
in Majori and Leilupe (both in

Cycling along Jūrmala beach

Windsurfing in Latvia

Jūrmala). The **Enri Tennis Centre** (*Kalnciema 207; tel: 6720 7757; www.enri.lv*) in Rīga has both indoor and outdoor courts, making it a good wet-weather option.

Ten-pin bowling

Ten-pin bowling is something of a national addiction, with centres located in or near the centre of many of Latvia's towns and cities. You can pick up flyers at the tourist office; alternatively, look out for the sign 'Boulings'. Two key locations are:

Bowlero
Lielirbes Iela 27, Rīga.
Tel: 6780 4600. www.bowlero.lv
Zemgale Sports Complex
Rīgas Iela 11, Jelgava.
Tel: 6300 7700. www.zemgale.info

WATERSPORTS

Kurzeme is one of the most popular regions in Latvia for watersports. Here you can take to the Tebra, Saka, Bārta and Tosele rivers, or the Engure, Kaņieris, Zvrigzdu, Usma, Pape and Sasmaka lakes in dugout canoes and kayaks. The Gauja River (*see p116*) is a prime kayaking spot, with the jaunt between Cēsis and Sigulda usually taking around two-and-a-half days. The Tourist Information Centre in Cēsis (*see p107*) and Sigulda (*see p110*) can give further information about sports in the Gauja Valley.

AIRBORNE ADVENTURES
Balloon trips

Weather conditions permitting, Traveller's Club **Altius** organises balloon flights in the Sigulda area that last around two hours, cover up to 20km (12 miles), and rise to a height of 1,000m (3,280ft). You need to book at least two days in advance.
Tel: 6761 1614; www.altius.lv

Skydiving/gliding

Although it claims to be Latvia's second international airport, the only flights (save the odd private landing) that Liepāja airport (*www.liepaja-airport.lv*) is currently handling are summer flights from Rīga and those made by skydivers and gliders. You can also skydive at the Cēsis Airfield. Ask at the Cēsis Tourist Information Centre (*see p107*) for details.

If you prefer risk-free 'skydiving', visit Sigulda's Aerodium, which boasts the only vertical wind tunnel in Eastern Europe (*Aerodium LGD atrakcijas, Sigulda; tel: 2838 4400; www.aerodium.lv*).

WINTER SPORTS
Ice skating
This is a great wet-weather activity, with indoor ice rinks located in Talsi, Liepāja and Ventspils, as well as other Latvian towns and cities.

Liepāja Ice Hall
Brīvības Iela 3/7.
Talsi Ice Hall
Kalna Iela 10.
Ventspils Ice Hall
Sporta Iela 7/9.

Skiing
Skiing is a popular winter sport in Latvia, but with its highest point at Gaiziņškalns standing just 312m (1,024ft) above sea level, the skiing is generally of the cross-country kind. Vidzeme is the largest skiing area and a large number of tracks are located in this region. There are a number of downhill stretches in Sigulda with descents of 200–300m (656–984ft), making them ideal for beginners. The

Skonto Rīga football stadium

Tourist Information Office in Sigulda (*see p110*) can provide further information.

Snowmobiles/tobogganing
In the winter you can sleigh in the Gauja Valley, which also has its own bobsleigh run – the bobsleigh team of the former USSR used to practise here (*see p111*). Tobogganing, though, is not confined to the colder months; summer runs are open in Sigulda and Pedvāle.

SPECTATOR SPORTS
Football
In recent years the popularity of football has risen and it now vies with ice hockey (*see pp160–1*) as the nation's favourite sport, largely due to the successes of the national team which qualified for Euro 2004 and helped halt Russia's 2006 World Cup ambitions. Skonto Rīga, who have begun to make small inroads into Europe such as beating top Scottish side Aberdeen, are at the pinnacle of Latvia's national game. FK Olympis have a stadium in Rīga, doubling your chances of catching a match in the capital. Ventspils and Liepāja also field their own teams, as do other towns.

Skonto Rīga
Melngaiļa Iela. www.skontofc.lv
FK Olympis
1 Augš Iela.
FK Ventspils
7-9 Sporta Iela. www.fkventspils.lv
FK Liepāja
Piejūras parks.

Ice hockey

Few European countries can say that their favourite sport is not football; Latvia is one of them. It would be no exaggeration to say that Latvia and its capital city are synonymous with ice hockey, or just 'hockey' as it is dubbed in local parlance; big victories are celebrated by fans sporting the distinctive maroon national colours partying through the city in jubilation.

The roots of ice hockey in Latvia can be traced back to the early 20th century when the locals played a game called 'bandy' on the ice, with competing teams using a ball rather than the standard puck that is used today. It took another two decades before 'Canadian hockey' with its puck came to Latvia, but the Latvian people soon made up for lost time and the sport quickly became very popular. Today there are 11 dedicated ice-rinks around the country, with over 3,000 active registered players.

During the Soviet era, when the communist bloc was one of the main powers in the sport, a number of Latvians starred as players in the USSR team.

The Latvian Hockey Federation was set up after independence and today there are eight main teams around the country. The best players are often lost to richer teams across the Atlantic, however, with Latvian players seizing the chance to play in the big-money National Hockey League. Players who have made the grade include Kārlis Skrastiņš and Sandis Ozoliņš, the latter the only Latvian player ever to have won the Stanley Cup, back in 1996, when he won a medal playing for Colorado Avalanche.

The Latvian National Team quickly proved its ability after independence; it entered the world top ten in 1997 and has pretty much stayed there ever

Ice hockey mascot

Ice hockey arena in Rīga, the venue for the World Championships held in 2006

since, with a highest ranking of seven. Despite promising performances, the Latvians have yet to make it to the medal stages of either the World or European championships, though individual results such as a group-stage World Championship win in 2000 over their arch rival, Russia, have been particularly welcomed by local supporters.

The high point in Latvia's fledgling history as an independent hockey nation came when it was awarded the right to host the 70th IIHF World Ice Hockey Championships for 2006. The event not only put Latvia in the spotlight, but also brought in massive investment in the form of facilities. The Skonto Stadium (the site of the Eurovision Song Contest in 2003) was upgraded to hold 6,500 spectators, and the brand-new 30 million euro Arena Rīga was opened in 2006 especially for the big event, with a capacity for 12,500 fans spread across a site that covers 58,000sq m (624,310sq ft). The slogan for the event summed things up perfectly for this hockey-obsessed city and country: 'The Championship in the City of Ice Hockey Fans.' Tickets for big games can be hard to get, but the maroon colours of the national side make good souvenirs and are on sale throughout Rīga and in other outlets around the country. The cuddly toy beavers – the symbol of the event – also make good presents for children back home.

Food and drink

Eating and drinking is an important part of Latvian life and culture, with substantial feasts accompanying every special occasion. Historically, Latvians relied on the land for their food; grains, peas, turnips, carrots and potatoes still form part of the staple diet. Beef, pork, poultry, horse meat and dairy products are also widely consumed. Game dishes of wild boar, duck, goose and venison are reserved for special occasions.

WHAT TO EAT AND DRINK
Food

Latvian cuisine tends to be simple. Boiled eggs, omelettes, bread, cheese, tomatoes and sausage are commonly eaten for breakfast. Traditionally lunch is the main meal of the day and it is usually eaten hot. A typical Latvian midday meal would consist of fried meat or fish accompanied by potatoes or rice and a creamy sauce or sour cream dressing. For Latvians living near the country's 494km (307-mile) coastline, fish is an integral part of the diet. In general, freshwater fish are regarded as more of a luxury. For those who wish to eat healthily, many eateries serve large and tasty salads (don't be fooled by claims that they are just accompaniments). At night Latvians may have another hot meal or a lighter snack. A must-try is the country's Laima chocolate.

Some dishes are seasonal, with bilberries, cranberries, loganberries, strawberries and raspberries going into summer cuisine, and mushrooms and nuts incorporated into autumn dishes. In winter hearty meat dishes and blood sausages find their way onto the menu. Smoked eel, cod, salmon, shrimps and trout are often available at any time of the year.

The German influence on Latvian food is at its most obvious in sauerkraut and yuletide gingerbread. Traditional Latvian cuisine includes hearty pork dishes like ribs, chops and even ears. *Pīrāgi* (bacon and onion buns) are a winter favourite. Most Latvians have a sweet tooth: honey and

COMMON FOODS

maize – bread	*olas* – eggs
sâls – salt	*pipari* – pepper
desa – sausage	*rupjmaize* – rye bread
siers – cheese	*zivis* – fish
zupa – soup	*vistu* – chicken
salâti – salad	*silîe* – herring
zutis – eel	*lasis* – salmon
forele – trout	*krçjums* – sour cream
frikadeles – meatballs	
manna – traditional semolina-like dessert	

sweet breads topped with berries, rhubarb and apple, or dried fruit and sweetened cottage cheese in the autumn and winter, are often eaten as a dessert or snack.

Vegetarians

Latvia is not an ideal destination for vegetarians as its culinary culture is based around meat and fish dishes. Even many seemingly vegetarian dishes may have meat stock or traces of meat. The best bets for vegetarians are salads and soup, which are available in most restaurants. In Rīga and other cities, vegetarian options are improving.

Drink

Tea and coffee, both usually drunk black, fruit juices and water are available all over Latvia, while beer is the country's most popular alcoholic drink (*see pp166–7*).

Many Latvians begin the day with a glass of milk, *rūgušpiens* (curdled milk) or *kefīrs* (cultured milk). Other traditional Latvian beverages include birch juice, *kvass* (a non-alcoholic drink made with yeast) and *medalus* (honey beer). The country also boasts its own particularly potent alcoholic liquor, Rīga Melnais Balzams or Rīga Black Balsams (*see pp40–41*).

WHERE TO EAT

In recent years Rīga has witnessed an explosion in the number and type of dining options, ranging from simple cafés and pizzerias to ethnic eateries

and more formal restaurants serving Latvian cuisine. Outside the capital, options are more limited, and hotel restaurants are often the best bet. Note that in 2006 smoking was banned in all bars and restaurants.

If you are on a self-catering visit, most villages have a shop where you can pick up fresh produce: in bigger settlements there will also be a market and at least one supermarket. In the restaurant listings given below, the star ratings indicate the average cost of a three-course meal for one excluding alcoholic drinks:

★   less than 10Ls (under $20)
★★   11–15Ls ($20–29)
★★★   16–24Ls ($30–40)
★★★★ over 25Ls (over $40)

A traditional restaurant in Liepāja

Food and drink

Rīga

Alus Sēta ★

This Latvian theme restaurant, complete with folk music and staff in traditional costume, serves inexpensive food and good beer in a hard-to-beat location. Locals and tourists flock here to dine on roast meat, hearty soups and bowls of delicious salad.
*Trigoņu Iela 6.
Tel: 6722 2431.*

Staburags ★

Excellent Latvian beer accompanies the heart-busting Latvian food at this popular restaurant. Portions are big but prices modest at a venue that is popular with both locals and tourists. Be warned, though – don't try and drink from the jugs at the table, as they are actually meant for your leftover bones!
Caka 55. Tel: 729 9787.

Soraksans ★★

Sushi restaurants are all the rage in the capital, and this Korean eatery serves the best in town. There is a wide range of other dishes to choose from, too.
Miesnieku Iela 12. Tel: 6722 9068.

Fellini ★★★

If you like Italian food, this is the place to come. With an Italian chef at the helm, the restaurant serves first-rate pasta dishes. Its truffles are a highlight.
*Berga Bazars, Marijas Iela 13.
Tel: 6728 4801.*

Bergs ★★★★

Widely considered Latvia's best dining restaurant, with immaculately turned-out staff, tasteful décor and first-class international food; a favourite with savvy locals.
*Hotel Bergs, Elizabetes Iela 83/85.
Tel: 6777 0957.*

Seasons ★★★★

A suitably grand restaurant in what many rate as the city's finest hotel. The menu changes with the seasons as the name suggests, making it a year-round favourite of the local business community right in the heart of the old town. A good place to sample fresh local produce.
*Pils 12, Hotel Grand Palace. Tel: 704 4000.
www.schlossle-hotels.com*

Zivju Restorans ★★★★

You can dine here on fresh fish straight from the restaurant's fishpond. Tender lobster, trout and eel are popular choices. The ideal venue for a romantic meal or a special treat.
*Vagnera Iela 4.
Tel: 6721 0087.*

Jūrmala

Al Thome ★★

Soak in Baltic Sea views while you dine on surprisingly authentic

Café in Cathedral Square, Rīga

Lebanese cuisine. Large salads will make you feel less guilty about tucking into crispy lamb.
Pilsoņu Iela 2, Majori. Tel: 6775 5755.

Sue's Asia ★★★

Enjoy Indian, Thai and Chinese dishes in pleasant Oriental surrounds. Be warned that the dishes haven't been watered down for Latvian tastes.
Jomas Iela 74, Majori. Tel: 6775 5900.

Caviar Club ★★★★

It might come at a price, but the experience of dining on fresh oysters, mouthwatering fish or rich game on the sea-view terrace is hard to beat.
Baltic Beach Hotel, Juras Iela 23/25, Majori. Tel: 6777 1100.

Kurzeme
Hotel Roja ★

The food served in Roja's only real dining option is a treat. Fresh and tasty salads and a divine fish platter are on offer alongside the usual grills.
Jūras Iela 6. Tel: 6323 2226.

Kalnavoti ★

Enjoy simple salads or heartier Latvian fare in a hard-to-beat setting. Dine on the balcony or in the riverside garden of this large wooden restaurant and B&B.
Signposted from the main road southeast of Koknese. Tel: 2911 7795.

Vecais Kapteinis (The Old Captain) ★★

Housed in a restored 18th-century building, this is a great place for traditional meat and fish dishes.
Dubelšteina 14. Liepāja.

Pastnieka Māja ★★★

This modern restaurant, dishing up Latvian staples alongside more innovative dishes,

deserves the esteem in which it is locally held.
Fr. Brivzemnieka Iela 53. Tel: 340 7521.

Vidzeme
Hotel Kolonna Cēsis ★★

The hotel's restaurant is the best place to dine in Cēsis. Lamb, beef and pork grills feature alongside fresh fish and 'specialities of the sea', a starter of smoked fish and langoustines.
Vienības Laukams 1, Cēsis. Tel: 6412 0122.

Pilsmuiža ★★

Enjoy the magnificent view of the old castle from this cosy restaurant housed in Sigulda's New Castle.
Pils Iela 16, Sigulda. Tel: 6797 4032.

Latvian seafood platter

Beer: Latvia's other gold

To say that Latvians love their beer (known locally as *alus*) is something of an understatement. After the Czechs, they are larger per capita drinkers of beer than in any other nation in Europe. Latvia is overflowing with

Cēsu beer from Cēsis

beer, whether it be in the bustling bars of trendy Rīga or in the more traditional countryside inns where you can relax in the sunshine and enjoy some of the country's finest beers. Latvian beer comes as something of a tonic for those used to tasteless multi-national brews; there is a real flavour and depth to the country's best beers despite some big foreign operators recently buying into domestic companies.

Beer drinking in the region dates back to the 13th century. Historical documents show there was a big dispute over the collection of hops for beer production in the Rīga area. By the end of the Middle Ages beer production was booming, with many people growing their own hops on a small scale at home. In the days of the Russian Tsars, when Latvia came under the direct rule of Russia, Rīga was known as 'Russia's Munich', such was the high regard in which the city's breweries were held. It is the Vidzeme town of Cēsis that today boasts the longest existent beer maker, Cēsu, which claims to have been brewing now for over four centuries.

These days things have been geared up, with large-scale

production and modern brewing facilities coming especially from two famous brands – the aforementioned Cēsu from Cēsis (now jointly owned by Scottish & Newcastle and Carlsberg) and Aldaris from Rīga (now owned by the Finnish company Olvi). These big players are backed by a number of smaller producers who create their own very distinctive flavours – some of these to look out for include Bauskas, Piebalgas and Rīgas. In 2000 the Union of Latvia Beer Makers had 16 members.

The main types of beer produced in the country today are *gaišs alus* and *tumšs alus*, the former a fizzy lager and the latter a darker drink more akin to stout. A tendency in recent years has been for the big two brewers to diversify into new products; Aldaris now brews 12 different types of beer in Latvia, including a light beer that is low on alcohol but still holds some real flavour, a trendy ICE beer that is popular with younger drinkers, and its landmark Zelta, an excellent 5.2 per cent golden all-rounder that is usually considered to be the country's most popular beer. The fainthearted might want to steer clear of Aldaris' Vanaga Stiprais, which packs a whopping 7 per cent alcohol and plenty of flavour. Whichever beer you try, you will be in good company in a country where it is as normal to see well-dressed office workers sharing cans of beer in a leafy park at lunchtime as it is to party into the small hours of the morning in a grungy Rīga beer hall with beer-drenched locals.

Latvia's favourite beer – Zelta

Hotels and accommodation

Until 1991 Latvia's accommodation facilities were limited and in poor condition, not really set up with today's demanding tourist in mind. Since independence, however, there has been a seismic shift; slick city hotels have opened in Rīga and other cities, and a proliferation of hotels, apartments, guesthouses, bed and breakfast places and youth hostels is available across the country.

The demand, though, can still outstrip the supply, so booking ahead is advised, particularly in the summer months. Prices in the capital are much higher than elsewhere, with double rooms in the Old Town typically starting at 60Ls ($100).

WHERE TO STAY

The following list of suggested options for accommodation will help you make an appropriate choice to suit your budget and holiday plans. The price guide is for a double room including breakfast:

★   Budget under 30Ls (under $60)
★★   Moderate/ Standard 30–59Ls ($60–115)
★★★   Expensive 60–100Ls ($115–190)
★★★★ Luxury over 100Ls (over $190)

Rīga

Hotel Kolonna Rīga ★★
This attractive boutique hotel is located in an old merchant's house. Rooms are modern and light; some also have impressive oak beams. A great option in this price category. To impress that special someone, book the penthouse and look out over the old town rooftops.
Tirgoņu 9. Tel: 6735 8254. www.hotel.kolonna.com

Centra ★★★
This funky boutique hotel is a stylish option handily located between the Old Town and the bus and railway stations. The 26 minimalist rooms are stylishly decorated, and have satellite TV and internet connections. Some of the rooms on the upper levels afford good views of the old town.
Audeju Iela 1. Tel: 6722 6441. www.centra.lv

Gutenbergs ★★★
Opened in 2001, this is a well-run hotel in an historic building in an Old Town location that could not be any more central. The best rooms tend to be in the newer wing. The rooftop terrace on the fifth floor is reason enough to visit, even if you are not staying.

Doma Laukums 1.
www.gutenbergs.lv

Konventa Seta ★★★
An atmospheric hotel
that is laid out in a
ramble of old convent
buildings in the heart of
the Old Town, offering
excellent value for
money. Rooms are bright
and comfortable with
most modern
conveniences. Highly
recommended.
Kaleju Iela 9/11.
Tel: 6708 7501.
www.konventa.lv

**Radisson SAS
Daugava** ★★★
The free airport transfer
helps make up for this
hotel's location on the
opposite bank of the

River Daugava. The
views of the Old Town
are superb across the
water, and the conference
and incentive facilities
are amongst the best in
Latvia.
Kugu Iela 24.
Tel: 6706 111.
www.radissonsas.com

Reval Hotel Latvija ★★★
If you're after a room
with a view, this sleek,
five-star hotel is hard to
beat. Book an upper-
floor room and request
an Old Town view.
With the Skyline Bar
(*see p148*), restaurants
and a casino on site, you
won't want to leave.
Elizabetes Iela 55.
Tel: 6777 2222.
www.revalhotels.com

Grand Palace ★★★★
Regarded by many as the
city's finest hotel, the
Grand Palace manages to
conjure up an old-world
feeling of luxury while
staying ahead of the
game with wi-fi available
in all the guest rooms.
Slick service, a sauna and
gym help complete the
picture. First class.
Pils Iela 12.
Tel: 6704 4000.
www.schlossle-hotels.com

Hotel Bergs ★★★★
Recently rated by *Conde
Nast* as one of the
world's best new
boutique hotels, this
slick operation in the
new town is indeed
impressive, both in terms
of the designer décor and

Enjoying a view of Rīga over a drink

Hotel Vila Joma in Jūrmala

the seamlessly smooth service.
Elizabetes Iela 83/85.
Tel: 6777 0900.
www.hotelbergs.lv

Jūrmala
Hotel Jūrmala
Spa ★★★

This large spa hotel offers a staggering range of health and beauty treatments including salt rooms, hydrotherapy and massage. Guestrooms are light and stylish.
Jomas Iela 47/49, Majori.
Tel: 778 4400.
www.hoteljurmala.com

Vila Joma ★★★

This boutique hotel, housed in a restored wooden villa, has just 16 rooms. Two minutes' walk from the beach.
Jomas Iela 90, Majori.
Tel: 6777 1999.
www.vilajoma.lv

Kurzeme
Hotel Fontaine ★

Run by a Danish pop star and his Latvian wife, this is one of the most surreally enjoyable places to stay in Latvia. Heavy-metal memorabilia clashes with Soviet-era kitsch in a collage that shouldn't work, but somehow does. It feels half student dorm/half boho hangout in Manhattan, but there is perhaps nothing like it anywhere else in Latvia, let alone Liepāja. Some

guests have reported that it can be too noisy to get a proper sleep.
Juras Iela 24, Liepāja.
Tel: 6342 0956.
www.fontaine.lv

Lacsetas ★

This rural retreat just a 10-minute drive from the historic town is the best staying option in Kuldīga. You can stay on a bed and breakfast basis or rent an entire timber-framed cottage in close proximity to a lake. The friendly owner, Artis, works in Kuldīga's tourist information centre, so if you haven't booked ahead you can always pop in to the office to see if he has

any rooms available.
Lacestas.
Tel: 6332 2259.
www.latviaholiday.com

Olimpiskā Centra Ventspils Viesnīca ★

The Olympic Centre hotel enjoys a great location near the beach and Ventspils' historic core, not to mention all the facilities at the Olympic Centre complex itself (including the water park). Constructed in 2003, it is one of the city's most modern hotel options. Good-value accommodation is available in single, double, triple and four-person rooms. Great for families.
Lilas Prospekts 33, Ventspils. Tel: 6362 8032.
www.ocventspils.lv

Talsi Hotel ★★

It may not be the most attractive accommodation option in Latvia, but the rooms are decent and it is this attractive town's only real hotel.
Kareivju Iela 16.
Tel: 6323 2022.
www.hoteltalsi.lv

Amrita Hotel ★★★

This Scandinavian-style business hotel is Liepāja's best accommodation option, benefiting from a central location and on-site bar and restaurant.
Rīgas Iela 7/9, Liepāja.
Tel: 6340 3434.
www.amrita.lv

Latgale
Atpūta Ezerzemēs ★★

This two-bedroomed log cabin with a cosy seating area and kitchen is a real gem. Overlooking tree-shrouded Lake Nirza, this rural haven in Raipole encapsulates the spirit of Latgale. Complete the experience by warming up in the sauna and then jumping into the lake. The owner, Lolita, speaks

German, Latvian and Russian. English speakers can book this and similar properties through Baltic Country Holidays.
Baltic Country Holidays Kugu Iela 11.
Tel: 6761 7600.
www.celotajs.lv

Vidzeme
Dikļi Palace Hotel ★★

For a real treat, book a room in this refurbished 15th-century manor house 20km (12 miles) from Valmiera. Recognised by the Latvian government as an historically important building back in 1998, today this country house impresses guests with its elegant rooms with period features. An on-site restaurant, sauna,

Typical Latvian rural guesthouse

steam room, Jacuzzi and plunge pool make it a perfect place for a romantic retreat.
Dikļu pagasts. Tel: 6420 7480. www.diklupils.lv

Guesthouse Lāču Miga ★★

Defining itself as a log cabin hotel situated in the heart of Gauja National Park, Lāču Miga has just 13 clean and simple guest rooms, some with nice designer touches. It also has a good restaurant and summer terrace, but the real winning element is its location.
Gaujas Iela 22, Līgatne.

Tel: 6415 3481. www.lacumiga.lv

Hotel Kolonna Cēsis ★★

Located in a refurbished mansion, this centrally located hotel boasts good-sized bedrooms and friendly and efficient staff, as well as the town's best restaurant. Wireless internet access and hairdryers (available from reception) are just some of the creature comforts.
Vienibas Laukums 1, Cēsis. Tel: 6412 0122. www.hotelcesis.lv

Hotel Sigulda ★★

Sigulda's best hotel is a successful blend of old and new. The modern guest rooms have been furnished to a high standard. Wireless internet access, a sauna, Jacuzzi and a first-rate restaurant provide the finishing touches.
Pils Iela 6, Sigulda. Tel: 6797 2263. www.hotelsigulda.lv

Līvkalns ★★

This attractive hotel close to the Satezele castle mound offers accommodation in 14 two-, three- and four-bed rooms. The restaurant serves up solid Latvian fare.
Pēteralas Iela, Sigulda. Tel: 6797 0916. www.livkalns.lv

Saulrieti ★★

Join the Rīgans as they flock out of the city during summer weekends to the nearby Vidzeme coastline. Just off the main Rīga–Tallinn highway is a lively bar-café in summer and a more tranquil retreat in the low season, with simple accommodation. Enjoy a drink on the

Mežotne Palace, now open as a hotel

terrace as you watch the
sun set over the Baltic
Sea, or relax in the
Jacuzzi.
Raiņa Iela 11, Saulkrasti.
Tel: 6795 1400.

Villa Alberta ★★
This cosy hotel has just
nine rooms, each of
which has been
individually styled,
although the theme
may not always be
immediately obvious.
The hotel also has a
Jacuzzi, sauna and small
fitness area.
Līvkalna Iela 10a,
Sigulda.
Tel: 6797 1060.
www.villaalberta.lv

Zemgale
Zemgale Hotel ★
This modern hotel
situated above a bowling
alley is a good choice for
families. The complex
also has tennis courts, an
informal café and an ice
hall where you can ice-
skate or play/watch ice
hockey. The guest rooms
are large and simply
furnished.
Rīgas Iela 11, Jelgava.
Tel: 6300 7707.
www.zemgale.info

Elegant bar at the Grand Palace

Youth hostels ★
Hostels affiliated with the
Latvian Youth Hostel
Association and
Hostelling International
can be found in Rīga,
Jūrmala, Kuldīga, Jelgava,
Ventspils and close to
Cēsis. Accommodation
ranges from doubles to
dormitory beds.
Standards in the hostels
tend to be good.
All the hostels can be
viewed on their
website and booked
through the central
reservation system.
17–2 Siguldas pr, Rīga.
Tel: 2921 8560.
www.hostellinglatvia.com

Mežotne Palace ★★
The regal Mežotne
Palace (*see pp86–7*)
has been turned
into an upmarket
hotel. The rooms are
decorated in classical
19th-century style, and
the bar and dining
areas are equally elegant.
When there isn't a
conference on, non-
residents can take a tour
of the second floor. The
family apartments for
three or four people are
especially good value
for money.
Mežotnes Pils.
Tel: 6396 0711.
www.mezotnespils.lv

Practical guide

Arriving

All foreign nationals need a valid passport or an acceptable national identity card to enter Latvia. Visa requirements vary between countries, with some people needing a visa, while others can stay for up to 90 days or a year without one. As Latvia adopts European Union policies, citizens from fellow EU countries are allowed to stay for as long as they want. At present, shorter-stay visa exemptions have been granted to Australia, Canada, the USA, New Zealand, Japan and most European nationals. Contact the Office of Citizenship and Migration Affairs for more information.
F-2, Alunāna 1, Rīga. Tel: 721 9656. www.pmlp.gov.lv

By air

Rīga international airport, located 13km (8 miles) from the capital, is served by direct flights from a large number of European countries including the UK, Ireland, the Netherlands, Spain, Germany, Denmark, Finland, Italy, Belarus, Russia, Norway, France, the Czech Republic, Sweden, Estonia, Austria, Lithuania, Poland and the Ukraine. There are also direct flights from Istanbul (Turkey), Tashkent (Uzbekistan), Tel Aviv (Israel) and New York. The majority of passengers travelling to Rīga from outside Europe will need to transfer between flights at one of the major European hubs. Departure tax is included in the price of your ticket. Rīga's airport has undergone major renovation, and is now modern and well equipped.
Tel: 6720 7009. www.riga-airport.com

By road

The main driving routes into Latvia are the Via Baltica, which runs south from Tallinn and north from Warsaw, Vilnius and Kaunas to Rīga; and the Via Hanseatica, which travels west from Berlin, Gdansk, Kaliningrad and Siauliai to Rīga. The capital is also easy to reach from Moscow in the east. Long-distance bus services run to Rīga from a number of German, Russian, Estonian and Lithuanian cities, as well as from London, Prague, Minsk (Belarus), Warsaw (Poland) and Kaliningrad (Russia). With budget airlines now linking Latvia and the UK, the 35-hour-plus coach journey is not as popular as it once was.

By train

Few international travellers arrive in Latvia by train as there are only limited services running from St Petersburg, Moscow and Kaunas (Lithuania) to Rīga.

By ferry

Rīga Jūras Līnja operates direct ferries between Rīga and Stockholm (Sweden). DFDS Torline runs a Rīga to Lübeck

(Germany) service, while Scandlines run services from Ventspils to Rostock (Germany), Nynäsham (Sweden) and Karlsham (Sweden). SCC Ferries operate a summer service (May–September) between Ventspils and Saarema in Estonia.

Rīga Jūras Līnja
Eksporta Iela 3a. http://pramis.rcc.lv

DFDS Torline
Zivju Iela. www.dfdstorline.lv

Scandlines
www.scandlines.lt

SCC Ferries
Ventspils Booking Office: Plosta Iela 5. Tel: 360 7184.
Kuressare Booking Office: Kohtu 1,

Kuressare, Estonia. Tel: +372 452 4376. www.slkferries.ee

Business etiquette in Latvia

Rīga is Latvia's financial and administrative hub, and the majority of business is conducted there. Latvia's accession to the EU in 2004 has seen an increase in the amount of international investment in the country. A younger generation of dedicated and career-minded Latvians is gradually moving into key positions, and their approach to business is a million miles away from that of the former Soviet Union. On the whole, business is conducted in the same way as it is in Paris, London or

Rīga is Latvia's business centre

any other major Western European city. One thing that many Latvians still need to work on, however, is punctuality.

If you are doing business in Latvia, you should wear formal attire: a suit and tie for men and smart conservative clothing for women. Latvians also tend to be immaculately presented, so make sure you have polished your shoes, have had a shave, and that your hair is neat and tidy. Meetings generally begin with a handshake, and any offer of a gift will be appreciated. If you are giving a gift to a stranger, stick to something fairly expensive and neutral, such as a bottle of single-malt Scotch whisky or an expensive bottle of wine. It is quite normal to conduct business over a leisurely lunch or dinner.

Camping

You don't have to travel too far to find a campsite in Latvia's rural areas; a large number of these facilities are signposted on the main roads. There also tends to be at least one official campsite located close to Latvia's main tourist centres. On the whole, camping grounds are pleasant, small and have reasonable facilities such as hot water and a small shop or café. Campers can also pitch their tents or park their trailers on a private field for a small charge (sometimes you will even be allowed to do this for free). If you want to stay warm at night, camping is only recommended between late May and early September. The Latvian Camping Association's website (*www.camping.lv*)

lists a number of campsites across the country, including Rīga City Camping. This list is far from comprehensive, however, and most people find somewhere to camp simply by following the signs sporting the picture of a tent or caravan.

Children

Latvia has a lot of attractions for children from kilometres of sandy beaches, city parks and playgrounds to waterparks and a wide range of outdoor activities (*see pp152–5*). Hotels generally cater for families and arrange extra beds for a small additional charge. Renting an apartment or log cabin in the countryside will ensure that every family member has plenty of space. In Latvian culture eating out is for adults, which means it can be tricky to find a child-friendly restaurant; children's portions are almost unheard off – so don't be shy to ask for an additional plate so that you can share a meal. Smoking is a particular problem, with many establishments not having a smoke-free area, although this is slowly beginning to change; some restaurants and cafés now have children's play areas.

Climate

Latvia has a temperate climate, with warm but short summers, mild springs, wet autumns and long cold winters. Most visitors travel to the country between May and September when temperatures average 16°C (61°F), and frequently reach the mid-20s (high 70s) in July and August. Between December and February temperatures rarely rise above freezing and can plummet as low as –10°C (14°F). Snowfall is common in the winter, but the days tend to be crisp and dry. Rainfall is fairly evenly spread through the rest of the year, with July being the wettest month.

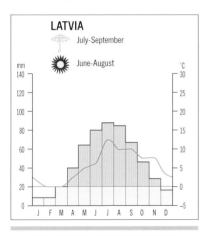

WEATHER CONVERSION CHART

25.4mm = 1 inch

°F = 1.8 × °C + 32

Crime

Petty and increasingly violent crime is unfortunately on the rise in Latvia, particularly in its larger towns and cities. By day, exercising sensible precautions like carrying valuables in inside pockets and carrying handbags securely should help prevent you from becoming a victim of crime.

CONVERSION TABLE

FROM	TO	MULTIPLY BY
Inches	Centimetres	2.54
Feet	Metres	0.3048
Yards	Metres	0.9144
Miles	Kilometres	1.6090
Acres	Hectares	0.4047
Gallons	Litres	4.5460
Ounces	Grams	28.35
Pounds	Grams	453.6
Pounds	Kilograms	0.4536
Tons	Tonnes	1.0160

To convert back, for example from centimetres to inches, divide by the number in the third column.

MEN'S SUITS

UK	36	38	40	42	44	46	48
Rest of Europe	46	48	50	52	54	56	58
USA	36	38	40	42	44	46	48

DRESS SIZES

UK	8	10	12	14	16	18
France	36	38	40	42	44	46
Italy	38	40	42	44	46	48
Rest of Europe	34	36	38	40	42	44
USA	6	8	10	12	14	16

MEN'S SHIRTS

UK	14	14.5	15	15.5	16	16.5	17
Rest of Europe	36	37	38	39/40	41	42	43
USA	14	14.5	15	15.5	16	16.5	17

MEN'S SHOES

UK	7	7.5	8.5	9.5	10.5	11
Rest of Europe	41	42	43	44	45	46
USA	8	8.5	9.5	10.5	11.5	12

WOMEN'S SHOES

UK	4.5	5	5.5	6	6.5	7
Rest of Europe	38	38	39	39	40	41
USA	6	6.5	7	7.5	8	8.5

At night, avoid getting excessively drunk, as alcohol has been a factor in a number of incidents when young men, in particular, have been robbed or assaulted. Try to avoid walking alone at night, especially on narrow, deserted or dark streets.

Rīga

Rīga has the highest level of crime in Latvia. Here the authorities have begun to take measures to prevent tourists being targeted by criminals, including having highly visible police officers (look out for the fluorescent jackets) patrol the city's streets after dark.

Taxis can be pre-booked to avoid being ripped off

Car crime

The police can do little to prevent your car from being broken into, vandalised or stolen. To minimise the risk, try to park your car in a secure car park and don't leave visible items inside. If the car stereo has a removable face, always take this with you.

Customs regulations

Travel from inside the European Union

On 1 May 2004 Latvia joined the European Union and now allows free movement of goods over its land borders with Lithuania and Estonia. Restrictions (albeit generous ones) still apply to those entering Latvia on flights from other EU countries: 800 cigarettes, 400 cigarillos, 200 cigars, 100kg of tobacco, 110 litres of beer, 90 litres of wine (up to 60 litres of this can be sparkling), 20 litres of liqueur, 10 litres of spirits, 10kg of coffee and 110 litres of non-alcoholic drinks can be brought into Latvia without incurring customs charges.

Travel from outside the European Union

For those flying in from a country that is not in the EU the duty-free limit is much smaller: 200 cigarettes (or the equivalent), 1 litre of spirits, 2 litres of liqueur and 50g of perfume, 250ml of eau de toilette and €175 of new or unused items intended for personal use.

Special measures

Until 2010 those flying to Austria, Germany, Denmark, Finland, Great Britain, Ireland and Sweden from Latvia can only take back an individual duty-free limit of 200 cigarettes. For more information, contact the Latvian State Revenue Service (*www.vid.gov.lv*).

Driving
Parking
Secure car parks can be found in Latvia's main tourist centres, towns and cities. However, spaces can be at a premium during July and August and parking may be restricted to one hour. Shopping centres and hotels also often have car parks, with others located just off the main highways that run along the coast. Blue signs with a white 'P' identify public car parks; restrictions are also clearly marked on signs, such as '1hr' or '24hrs'. If payment is required there will usually be a ticket kiosk or machine nearby.

Breakdown
Anyone driving a hired car should call the rental company if it breaks down. The Auto-Moto Society of Latvia (*www.lamb.lv*) provides breakdown assistance. LAMB cardholders are entitled to free or discounted service in Rīga and across the country, depending on the level of cover purchased (10–35Ls). In case of a breakdown, call *1888*.

Car hire
A number of international car rental companies have offices at Rīga's international airport. Europcar (*www.europcar.lv*) and Hertz (*www.hertz.lv*) have branches in Rīga as well as in Liepāja and Ventspils. In order to rent a car in Latvia, you need to have held a valid driving licence for at least two years. You will also need a passport (or national identity card) and a credit card for the deposit. Age restrictions apply, with the driver needing to be at least 21 years old, although some companies have raised this limit to 23 or 25 years. Vehicles can generally be rented on a daily or weekly basis, and prices tend to be high.

Documents and insurance
Theft and collision damage waiver insurance is often included in the price of the car hire, while personal accident cover will generally incur an extra charge. It is essential to check what is covered by the insurance policy, and any excess charges, prior to your hire.

The Cyrillic names have been erased from this sign

When you rent a car in Latvia you will be given the car's registration and insurance documents, which will need to be produced along with your driving licence and passport or national identity card if you are stopped by the police. Do not leave them in the car when it is unattended. Those driving private vehicles must also keep all their documents with them, including evidence that they are covered by third-party insurance.

Fuel

Unleaded fuel and diesel are available at most petrol stations. In large urban centres filling stations have multiple self-service pumps; in rural areas they may well be run-down, have one pump and insist that you pay in advance (if you overpay you will not get a refund). Don't attempt a long journey if you are low on fuel, as it may be some time before you come across a petrol station.

Traffic regulations

Latvians drive on the right, and it is compulsory to wear seatbelts in the front and back. Headlights should be turned on at all times. Speed limits are 50kph (31mph) in towns and 90kph (56mph) on highways, unless there are signs telling you otherwise. The blood alcohol limit is 0.05 per cent, but it is much safer to avoid alcohol altogether when driving. Police speed traps are common and on-the-spot fines are issued for minor traffic violations and speeding offences.

Roads

Latvia's roads may not be up to standard, with surfaces on highways varying from new tarmac to sealed roads riddled with potholes and compacted dirt tracks. In the countryside minor roads are often very narrow, muddy and strewn with pebbles. During heavy rain the roads can be particularly hazardous. On the upside, the roads are generally quiet and traffic-free, particularly outside the main tourist season.

Electricity

Latvia uses a 220V, 50Hz electrical system, with two-pin, round-pronged European plugs. Remember to pack European plug adaptors or to pick them up at your departure airport, as these are not commonly sold inside the country.

Embassies and consulates

All the foreign embassies and consulates listed here are in Rīga.
Canada *Baznīcas Iela 20–22. Tel: 6781 3945. www.dfait-maeci.gc.ca*
Ireland *Valdemāra 21.*
Tel: 6703 5286.
UK *Alunāna Iela 5. Tel: 6777 4700. www.britain.lv*
USA *Raiņa Bulvāris 7. Tel: 6703 6200. www.usembassy.lv*

Emergency telephone numbers
Ambulance *03*
Fire *01*
Police *02*

Health

The European Health Insurance Card, which replaced the E111 in 2005, entitles those from other EU countries, as well as citizens of Iceland, Liechtenstein, Norway and Switzerland, to free emergency health care in Latvia. This reciprocal health agreement does not, however, cover the cost of repatriation and non-emergency care. It is important to take out travel insurance that gives you adequate health cover prior to visiting the country.

You do not need any special vaccinations to visit Latvia. However, if you are planning on spending prolonged periods in forested areas, you should consider being vaccinated against tick-borne encephalitis. It is wise to take simple precautions if you are in wooded areas, like wearing long sleeves and trousers, applying insect repellent and checking for ticks at the end of the day. Large towns and cities in Latvia will have either a hospital or a health centre, although the standards of care are sometimes below those offered in most Western countries.

Maps

Most tourist offices provide decent maps of towns and cities. If you are planning to drive in Latvia you will need to purchase a detailed map, as road signs are sometimes confusing or nonexistent. Maps can be bought on the internet from Amazon (*www.amazon.co.uk*) prior to your departure, or at petrol stations, bookshops and tourist offices in Latvia.

Media

Printed media

If you are looking for English-language news check out the weekly *Baltic Times* (*www.baltictimes.com*) which covers news in Latvia, Lithuania and Estonia, and the monthly Latvia-centric *Baltic Guide* (*www.balticguide.com*). Foreign language newspapers may also be available in hotels and some outlets in Rīga. The main Latvian daily, *Diena* (*www.diena.com*), has a Latvian and a Russian edition. These can all be read online.

Television

Unless you are staying in a hotel with satellite television, your viewing choices will be strictly limited. The two state-run Latvijas Televizija (Latvian

An old street in Kuldīga, a quiet place to cycle or stroll

Language

Latvian is the official language of the country, although significant minorities speak Russian and German. In Rīga and in higher-grade hotels, the staff will also be able to speak English, as can a large proportion of the younger population. Latvian is a complex Indo-European language that can leave you tripping over your tongue. Learning some key phrases will set you in good stead and encourage Latvians who are not confident to speak to you in English.

PRONUNCIATION
Vowels

a as the u in hut
ā as the a in rather
ai as the i in hike
e as the e in vet
ē as the a in rare
i as the i in hit
ī as the ee in feet
o as uo (more like aw in foreign words)
u as the oo in soot
ū as the oo in brood

Consonants

English pronunciation: b, d, f, g, h, k, l, m, n, p, s, t, v and z.

c as ts
č as ch
ǧ as the dj sound in endure
j as the y in you
ķ as the tj sound in chew
ļ as the lli sound in billion
ņ as the ni sound in reunion
š as sh
ž as the s in division
r is trilled

GREETINGS

hello	sveiki/labdien
goodbye	uz redzēšanos
good morning	labrīt
good evening	labvakar
good night	ar labu nakti

EVERYDAY EXPRESSIONS

yes	jā
no	nē
please	lūdzu
thank you	paldies

excuse me	atvainojiet/Lūdzu
I do not speak Latvian	es nerunāju latviski
I do not understand	nesaprotu
how much?	cik?
expensive	dārgs
toilet	tualete

TIME

today	šodien
yesterday	vakar
tomorrow	rīt

DAYS OF THE WEEK

Sunday	Svïtdiena
Monday	Pirmdiena
Tuesday	Otrdiena
Wednesday	Trešdiena
Thursday	Ceturtdiena
Friday	Piektdiena
Saturday	Sestdiena

MONTHS OF THE YEAR

January	Janvâris
February	Februâris
March	Marts
April	Aprîlis
May	Maijs
June	Jûnijs
July	Jûlijs
August	Augusts
September	Septembris
October	Oktobris
November	Novembris
December	Decembris

NUMBERS

1	viens
2	divi
3	trîs
4	âetri
5	pieci
6	seši
7	septiņi
8	astoņi
9	deviņi
10	desmit
20	divdesmit
30	trîsdesmit
40	četrdesmit
50	piecdesmit
100	simts
1000	tûkstotis

EATING AND DRINKING

FOOD

cake	kūka
ice cream	saldejums
meat	gala
vegetables	saknes
fruit	augli
egg	ola
bread	maize
rye bread	rupjmaize
apple	âbols
orange	apelsîns
sausage	desa
potatoes	kartupeli
cabbage	kâposti
cherry	kirsis
cheese	siers

DRINKS

coffee	kafija
tea	teja
water	ûdens
beer	alus
wine	vîns
milk	piens
juice	sula

A board displaying the exchange rate

Television) stations broadcast the majority of their programmes in Latvian, with around 20 per cent being in Russian. TV3 is owned by a Swedish company but the majority of its programmes are geared towards Latvian speakers. Euronews, Eurosport and BBC World are amongst the most commonly available English-language satellite channels.

Radio

The main Radio Skonto station plays a wide range of music and covers topical news. Other popular radio stations, such as Super FM, Mix FM and Radio SWH, broadcast an intriguing or, depending on your view, annoying mix of English-language chart toppers, Euro pop (with nonsensical lyrics in English) and Russian pop.

Money matters

Currency

The official currency of Latvia is the lat – a decimal currency with 100 santīmi to the lat. Latvian notes are printed in denominations of 5, 10, 20, 50, 100 and 500 lati, with 1, 2, 5, 10, 20 and 50 santīmi coins.

Banks

All towns and cities in Latvia have at least one centrally located bank. Most open Monday–Friday, 9am–6pm, and on Saturday mornings. The majority of banks offer a currency exchange service and have ATMs (automated teller machines) that accept Cirrus and Maestro or Mastercard and Visa.

Currency exchange

Banks, post offices and exchange offices, as well as some hotels and shops, will change foreign currency for lati. US dollars and euros are the easiest currencies to exchange. Some banks will also exchange traveller's cheques, but the commission tends to be higher.

Credit cards/debit cards

Visa and Mastercard/Eurocard are the most commonly accepted credit cards in Latvia, with Electron, Maestro and Cirrus debit payments also accepted in many locations. It is a good idea to keep a record of your card issuer's international telephone number in case it gets lost or stolen. Many retailers require signatures even with PIN cards.

Opening hours

The opening hours given here are a guide only.

Banks

Monday–Friday 9am–6pm. Some open on Saturday mornings, or all day.

Offices

Monday–Friday 9am–6pm.

Post offices

Monday–Friday 8am–6pm (some open until 8pm or 10pm). Weekend times vary.

Shops

Monday–Saturday 10am–8pm and Sunday 10am–4pm.

Grocery shops/supermarkets

Monday–Sunday 10am–8pm (sometimes 10pm).

Cafés and restaurants

Monday–Sunday 10am–8pm (often close much later in the cities).

Bars

Monday–Sunday 10am–midnight (often close much later in the cities).

Police

Dial *02* from a landline or *112* from a mobile to call the Latvian police. The police must be called in the event of a road accident. In Rīga you may see police wearing fluorescent jackets patrolling the streets at night.

Post offices

All towns, cities and larger villages in Latvia will have a post office and they are frequently signposted on the main road; look out for the sign of a sealed envelope. Post boxes are yellow and marked *pasts* (post). In larger post offices you can make international phone calls, change money and buy postcards, as well as posting letters and parcels. Opening times vary, but most are open all day during the week and on Saturday mornings.

Public holidays

I January New Year

March/April Easter Sunday

1 May Labour Day

May Mothering Sunday

23 and 24 June Līgo (Midsummer)

11 November Lāčplēsis Day

18 November The day of the proclamation of the Republic of Latvia

24–26 December Christmas

31 December New Year's Eve

Public transport

Inner-city transport

The majority of tourist sights located in Latvia's cities and towns can be easily explored on foot.

Buses, trams and trolleybuses

Rīga has an efficient network of buses, trams and trolleybuses, and bus services in Ventspils and Liepāja are decent. The latter also has a solitary tram route, but this will probably be of little use to most visitors. In Latvia's urban centres you will also see taxis and minibuses, called *mikroautobuss* or *taksobuss*. If you want to catch a minibus, simply wait at the bus stop.

Taxis

Taxis can be hailed from the street or pre-booked by phone. Outside Rīga taxi drivers are unlikely to speak English. Unlicensed taxis operating in large cities should be avoided.

Long-distance travel

Long-distance travel in Latvia can be done by rail, bus or plane. The most useful train routes for tourists are the ones that link Rīga to Jūrmala and Jelgava. Trains also run between Rīga and Sigulda, although the journey is shorter by bus. Details of rail and selected bus timetables in Latvia can be found in the *Thomas Cook European Rail Timetable*, available to buy online from *www.thomascookpublishing.com*, from Thomas Cook branches in the UK, or *tel: 01733 416477*.

The country's long-distance bus network is more comprehensive, with services connecting the major urban centres, although they don't always take the most direct route, such as the bus between Ventspils and Liepāja which goes through Kuldīga.

Rīga's *Autoosta* (central bus station) is a useful source of information for those planning to travel by bus (*Prāgas Iela 1. Tel: 900 009 (0.24Ls/min). www.autoosta.lv*). On the whole, buses run frequently and are quicker than trains.

Domestic flights

Latvia's first scheduled domestic commercial flight connecting Rīga to Liepāja took off in 2005.

Student and youth travel

If you are travelling on a budget in Latvia there are a number of private hostels. Hostelling Latvia (*see p173*) lists HI hostels on its website, and local

Līgatne ferry, an old-world mode of transport in Vidzeme

tourist offices will tell you about private hostels. There is also an STA travel agency in Rīga (Kolumbus), which helps arrange cheaper travel for students and people under the age of 26.

An International Student Identity Card (ISIC) is the best way to prove your student status, and will give you discounts on a range of services and entrance prices including to some museums and nightclubs.

Kolumbus Raiņa Bulvāris 21, Rīga. Tel: 6721 2121. www.statravel.lv

Sustainable tourism

Thomas Cook is a strong advocate of ethical and fairly traded tourism and believes that the travel experience should be as good for the places visited as it is for the people that visit them. That's why we're a firm supporter of The Travel Foundation, a charity that develops solutions to help improve and protect holiday destinations, their environment, traditions and culture. To find out what you can do to make a positive difference to the places you travel to and the people who live there, please visit *www.thetravelfoundation.org.uk*

Telephones

Most of Latvia's payphones are operated by a *telekarte* (phone card), which can be purchased anywhere displaying the *telekarte* sign, including post offices, kiosks and shops. *Telekartes* come in 2-, 3- and 5-lati denominations. For overseas calls

purchase the most expensive card. Most hotels will have telephones that allow international direct dialling, but calls will be charged at a premium rate.

International dialling code

Latvia's international dialling code is *371* and there are no city codes. To call a Latvian number from abroad, first dial your country's exit code followed by the *371*. You will then need to dial all eight digits of the Latvian telephone number. Eight-digit numbers began replacing seven-digit numbers midway through 2007. The process should be complete by July 2008.

Here are the main country codes, should you want to make an international call from Latvia.

USA and Canada *00 1*
UK *00 44*
Ireland *00 353*
Australia *00 61*
New Zealand *00 64*

Domestic calls

When making a telephone call inside Latvia you simply need to dial the 8-digit number; this also applies when you are ringing a Latvian mobile phone.

Due to the time taken to change over from 7- to 8-digit phone numbers, some 7-digit numbers were still in use at the time of writing. If you come across a 7-digit number that no longer works, prefix it with a 6. Mobile telephone numbers, which used to begin 9, are now prefixed with a 2.

Time

GMT + 2 hours

Tipping

Some restaurants add a 10 per cent service charge to the bill and customers are often advised of this on the menu. It is considered polite to tip 10–15 per cent if service is not included. However, if you are just having a drink at the bar there is no need to leave a tip. You should also tip taxi drivers around 10 per cent.

Toilets

Toilets in cafés, restaurants and hotels are generally clean, flushable and have toilet paper. The same, unfortunately, cannot be said about the public toilets, which are sometimes little more than a filthy hole in the ground; this also applies to the triangular wooden cabins in the car parks at most tourist attractions and beaches. If you are using a café toilet it is polite to buy a drink first; you may also need to ask for the key to unlock the door.

Tourist information

Before travelling to Latvia you can obtain travel information from the Latvian Tourist Office's website *www.latviatourism.lv*

Tourist offices in Latvia

Aizpute: Skolas Iela. Tel: 6344 8880. www.aizpute.lv
Bauska: Rātslaukums 1. Tel: 6392 3797. www.tourism.bauska.lv

Cēsis: Pils Laukums 1.
Tel: 6412 1815. www.cesis.lv
Dundaga: Pils Iela 14. Tel: 6323 2293. www.dundaga.lv
Jēkabpils: Brivības Iela 140/142.
Tel: 6523 3822.
Jelgava: J. Čakstes bulvāris 7.
Tel: 6302 3874. www.jelgava.lv
Jūrmala: Lienas Iela 5.
Tel: 6714 7900. www.jurmala.lv
Kuldīga: Baznīcas Iela 5.
Tel: 6332 2259. www.kuldiga.lv
Liepāja: Rožu Laukums 516.
Tel: 6348 0808. www.liepaja.lv
Limbaži: Burtnieku Iela 5.
Tel: 6407 0608. www.limbazi.lv
Ludza: Baznīca Iela 42.
Tel: 6570 720. www.ludza.lv
Mērsrags: Dzintaru Iela 1/9.
Tel: 6323 5470. www.mersrags.lv
Rīga: Rāstlaukums 6.
Tel: 6703 7900.
www.rigatourism.com
Roja: Selgas Iela 33. Tel: 6326 9594.
www.roja.lv
Sabile: Pilskalna Iela 6. Tel: 6325 2344.
www.sabile.lv
Sigulda: Valdemara Iela 1a.
Tel: 6797 1335. www.sigulda.lv
Smiltene: Dāra Iela 3. Tel: 6470 7575.
www.smiltene.lv
Talsi: Liēla Iela 19-21. Tel: 322 4165.
www.talsi.lv
Tukums: Pils Iela 3. Tel: 6312 4451.
www.tukums.lv
Valka: Rīgas Iela 22. Tel: 6472 5522.
www.valka.lv
Ventspils: Tirgus Iela 7.
Tel: 6362 2263. www.ventspils.tourism.lv

Travellers with disabilities

In recent years Latvia has been working hard to make life easier for people with disabilities, with the most significant improvements being provision of special parking spaces, accessible toilets and hotels that allow wheelchair access to both communal areas and guest rooms. This is, however, by no means true for most destinations or establishments; cobbled streets, hotels with no lifts and sand dunes without ramps pose the biggest obstacles. In Jūrmala the authorities have introduced wooden ramps to allow every visitor the chance to access the beach. Travellers with disabilities should contact the Latvian National Tourist Office for further advice prior to their departure.

Practical guide

The tourist office in Jūrmala can give you information on performances at Dzintari Concert Hall

Index

Acknowledgements

Thomas Cook wishes to thank the photographer ROBIN McKELVIE for the loan of the photographs in this book, to whom the copyright belongs (except the following):

LATVIAN TOURISM BUREAU 92, 96, 121, 126, 127, 170, 189

CHRISTOPHER VOITUS 55

HARALD HANSEN 95

WORLD PICTURES/PHOTOSHOT 25, 59, 61, 83, 85, 100, 155, 164, 175

For CAMBRIDGE PUBLISHING MANAGEMENT LIMITED:
Project editor: Karen Beaulah
Typesetter: Trevor Double
Proofreader: Jan McCann
Indexer: Karolin Thomas

SEND YOUR THOUGHTS TO
BOOKS@THOMASCOOK.COM

We're committed to providing the very best up-to-date information in our travel guides and constantly strive to make them as useful as they can be. You can help us to improve future editions by letting us have your feedback. If you've made a wonderful discovery on your travels that we don't already feature, if you'd like to inform us about recent changes to anything that we do include, or if you simply want to let us know your thoughts about this guidebook and how we can make it even better – we'd love to hear from you.

Send us ideas, discoveries and recommendations today and then look out for your valuable input in the next edition of this title.

Emails to the above address, or letters to Travellers Series Editor, Thomas Cook Publishing, PO Box 227, Coningsby Road, Peterborough PE3 8SB, UK.

Please don't forget to let us know which title your feedback refers to!